Computer Assisted Instruction for Health Professionals

A Guide to
Designing and Using
CAI Courseware

Computer Assisted Instruction for Health Professionals

A Guide to Designing and Using CAI Courseware

Diane M. Billings, R.N., Ed. D.
Associate Professor of Nursing
Indiana University School of Nursing
Indianapolis, Indiana

 APPLETON-CENTURY-CROFTS/Norwalk, Connecticut

Copyright © 1986 by Appleton-Century-Crofts
A Publishing Division of Prentice-Hall

86 87 88 89 90 / 10 9 8 7 6 5 4 3 2 1

Prentice-Hall of Australia, Pty. Ltd., Sydney
Prentice-Hall Canada, Inc.
Prentice-Hall Hispanoamericana, S.A., Mexico
Prentice-Hall of India Private Limited, New Delhi
Prentice-Hall International (UK) Limited, London
Prentice-Hall of Japan, Inc., Tokyo
Prentice-Hall of Southeast Asia (Pte.) Ltd., Singapore
Whitehall Books Ltd., Wellington, New Zealand
Editora Prentice-Hall do Brasil Ltda., Rio de Janeiro

Library of Congress Cataloging-in-Publication Data

Billings, Diane McGovern.
    Computer assisted instruction for health professionals.

    Includes index.
    1. Medicine—Computer assisted instruction.
2. Computer assisted instruction—Programming.
I. Title. [DNLM: 1. Computer Assisted Instruction—
methods. 2. Health Occupations—education.
W 18 B598c]
R837.C6B55 1986   610'.7'8   86-10725
ISBN 0-8385-1221-6

Design: M. Chandler Martylewski

```
10      REM     Dedication
20      PRINT   "Thank you"
30      PRINT   "Dick"
40      GO TO   20
50      END
```

Contents

Preface

The current information explosion in the health care field increases the responsibility of health care professionals and educators for efficient knowledge dissemination and cost effective education and training. Computer assisted instruction (CAI) is one instructional medium that can be used by health care professionals such as nurses, physicians, dentists, pharmacists, occupational therapists, physical therapists, respiratory therapists, and radiologic technologists for transmitting knowledge and skills to students, practitioners, and clients. As the computer becomes an integral component of educational settings, health care agencies, offices and homes, health care professionals and educators must be prepared to use CAI and develop CAI courseware. The purpose of this book is to provide a guide for using and designing computer assisted instruction for health care professionals.

Health care professionals and educators are assuming and will assume the role of CAI author because their experience with learners and content and clinical expertise are essential to courseware development. CAI authors may be members of a CAI design team where instructional designers and computer programmers support content expertise. Recently, however, several authoring systems have been developed for the specific needs of health care disciplines. These systems decrease courseware development time and personnel and will facilitate the development of CAI by health care professionals.

This guide is written for health care professionals who will be designing their own courseware or serving on design teams. It bridges the gap between content expert and CAI author by providing guidelines for instructional design. The design process begins by reviewing principles of teaching and learning essential for designing CAI (Chap. 3) and continues by describing a systematic approach and tools used in developing a CAI lesson (Chap. 4). The design model is implemented in subsequent chapters which detail designs of four popular CAI strategies: drill and practice (Chap. 7), tutorials (Chap. 8), simulations (Chap. 9), and computer administered tests (Chap. 10). Chapters on screen design (Chap. 5) and authoring tools (Chap. 6) provide information for translating lesson plans to instructionally motivating screen displays.

This guide is also written for the health professional who will be using CAI with students in professional education, colleagues in continuing professional education or staff development, and clients. The first chapter provides an overview of computer assisted instruction, advantages and disadvantages, and the potential for use in a variety of instructional strategies. Chapter 2 provides guidelines for determining the instructional need for CAI and identifying and selecting appropriate CAI courseware. Chapter 11 gives suggestions for using CAI in instructional settings and Chapter 12 provides information about evaluating instructional effectiveness.

This book is written as a practical guide for using and designing CAI. Flowcharts, storyboards and step-by-step guides for writing instructional specifications demonstrate design procedures. Screen designs, evaluation tools, figures and tables are provided to stimulate creativity. Each chapter concludes with a checklist to summarize and to serve as a working tool for the CAI user and author.

All instructional design efforts are enhanced by colleague support and review; those who have contributed to this guide are acknowledged here. Thanks are extended to Terri Keating, R.N., M.S.N., and Lillian Yeager, R.N., M.S.N., for reviewing the manuscript as members of the "target audience;" Steve Snideman and Lorri Hegstad, R.N., Ph.D., content experts; Steffani White, typist and graphic artist; Hal Keith, artist; and Richard Billings, "language expert" and computer consultant. Thanks, too, to the editorial staff at Appleton-Century-Crofts, Stu Horton, Kathy Drasky and Jennifer Schwartz.

Computer Assisted Instruction for Health Professionals

A Guide to
Designing and Using
CAI Courseware

1

Computer Assisted Instruction

I. Computer Based Instruction
   A. Computer Managed Instruction
      1. Computer Based Training
   B. Computer Assisted Instruction
      1. CAI and Video
      2. CAI and Slides
      3. CAI and Audiotape
      4. CAI and Training Equipment
   C. Intelligent Computer Assisted Instruction
II. CAI and Hardware, Software, Courseware
   A. Hardware
      1. Input Devices
      2. Central Processing Unit
      3. Output Devices
      4. Selecting Hardware
   B. Software
   C. Courseware
III. CAI and Instruction
   A. Diagnosing Learning Needs
   B. Presenting Instruction
   C. Enriching Instruction
   D. Remediating Instruction
   E. Evaluating Instruction
IV. CAI Instructional Strategies
   A. Drill and Practice
   B. Tutorial
   C. Simulation
   D. Gaming
   E. Problem Solving
   F. Model Building
   G. Testing
V. Advantages and Disadvantages of CAI
   A. Advantages
      1. Individualized Instruction
      2. Quality Instruction
      3. Time Efficiency and Effectiveness

As computers become an increasingly popular medium of instruction, health professionals must be prepared to maximize their use by understanding the medium and designing, selecting, using, and evaluating computer assisted instruction (CAI) for professional education, staff development, continuing education, and for client instruction. After reading this chapter you will be able to define computer assisted instruction, differentiate hardware, software, and courseware, state instructional uses of CAI, identify CAI instructional strategies, and cite advantages and disadvantages of this medium of instruction. You will also be able to recognize future uses of CAI and the implications for education.

COMPUTER BASED INSTRUCTION

Computer based instruction (CBI), often called computer assisted learning (CAL), is a general term for the use of computers in instruction. Computer managed instruction and computer assisted instruction, on the other hand, have more specific definitions (Fig. 1–1).

Computer Managed Instruction

Computer managed instruction (CMI) refers to the potential of the computer to manage instruction or guide learners through a lesson, module,

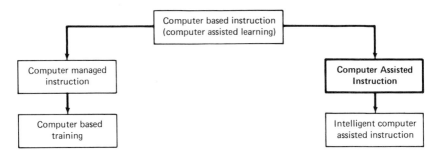

Figure 1-1. Computer based instruction and CAI.

course, or curriculum. Here the computer can present the course syllabus or learning objectives, provide instruction, schedule films, field trips, or clinical experiences, administer tests, and keep a record of the learner's assignments and course progress. Messages can also be left by the instructor for the student or by the student for the instructor. The emphasis is on the management of instruction, testing, and record keeping. Reports can be generated for the student and the instructor.

Computer managed instruction is used in health care education settings to guide learners through independent study courses in undergraduate and graduate education. It is also used in orientation, staff development, or continuing education to provide instruction and monitor attendance.

Computer Based Training. Computer based training (CBT) is another term used to describe the computer's role in managing instruction. CBT is used in training settings where learning tasks are identified, objectives determined, and mastery performance levels established. Here there is an emphasis on skill aquisition and performance.

In health care settings CBT is oriented toward the needs of a particular health care agency. It is used, for example, in general orientation to an agency or in specialized orientation programs such as a critical care course where all employees must meet specified training standards for work performance.

Computer Assisted Instruction

CAI is the process of providing written and visual information in a logical sequence by the computer. The focus is on instruction. CAI as a medium of instruction has become increasingly popular as microcomputers are available in universities and colleges, learning centers, health care agencies, offices, and homes.

CAI is not dependent on the size of the computer (microcomputer,

minicomputer, or mainframe). CAI can also be used with several ad-
junctive media to enhance visual and auditory capacity.

CAI and Video. CAI can be used with videotape or videodisk to add
motion and visual reality to instruction. The marriage of the computer
and video is known as interactive video and increases the interactivity of
the videotape or videodisk (Fishman, 1984).

Although both videodisk and videotape can be used as adjuncts to
CAI, there are advantages and disadvantages of each. The videodisk can
be accessed at any point in the program, thus increasing the routes by
which the learner can approach the video. This feature is particularly
significant in simulations in which several options for courses of action
are presented to the learner. Videodisks are more expensive to purchase,
but the rapid access contributes significantly to the efficiency and aesthetics of a lesson.

Videotapes may also be used with the computer. Many health care
agencies and schools already have videotapes which they have developed
or purchased and these can be used with the computer. Videotapes, however, can only be accessed in a sequential manner, thus limiting their use
or subjecting the viewer to lengthy searches for the appropriate segment
used in the lesson.

CAI and Slides. The computer can also be used with slides. The computer can control the presentation or direct the learner to view selected
slides. The advantages of using slides to provide realism can be out-
weighed by the difficulty of accessing slides and the need for two screens
(one for the computer and one for the slides).

CAI and Audiotape. Some instruction, such as auscultation or inter-
viewing skills, is enhanced by audio. It is possible to add audiotapes to
the CAI lesson.

CAI and Training Equipment. CAI can also be coupled with equipment
or training mannequins (Schwartz, 1984). ECG monitors or laboratory
equipment for example may be useful adjuncts to a CAI lesson. In one
elaborate use of CAI the computer is used with the cardiopulmonary
resuscitation mannequin to present the basic cardiac rescuer course (Hessinger, 1981). Sensors are attached to the mannequin and feedback can
be given on the computer about skill performance.

Intelligent Computer Assisted Instruction

Intelligent computer assisted instruction (ICAI) uses artificial intelligence
programming techniques to diagnose human problem-solving processes

and to give prescriptions for remediation. ICAI currently involves complex programming structures and the support of a mainframe computer. It can be anticipated, however, that ICAI will become more sophisticated as experience and consumer demand dictate. Models of the expert problem solver, clinician, or diagnostician will then be available to guide the learning of the beginning health care professional.

CAI AND HARDWARE, SOFTWARE, COURSEWARE

CAI requires the use of hardware, software, and courseware. Considerations for purchase and use of these must be made at the outset and the CAI user or author should be familiar with current availability of hardware, software, and courseware for his or her particular needs.

Hardware

The computer is a piece of electronic equipment used to process data. The components of the computer, known as hardware, include an input device, the central processing unit, and output devices.

Input Devices. Input devices are used to enter data into the computer. The most common input device is the keyboard on which the learner enters responses by typing. Other input devices are light pens, joysticks, a mouse, or a touch screen. Sophisticated systems use voice recognition as an input device.

Central Processing Unit. The central processing unit, or CPU, executes the input and output operations and processes data. The main memory for data processing resides within the CPU.

Output Devices. Output devices are used to transmit data to the user for display or to a disk or printer for storage. Output devices include the monitor or video display terminal (VDT) which is also known as the cathode ray tube (CRT), printer, and disk.

Selecting Hardware. If you are considering using or designing CAI it is important to select hardware prior to CAI development (Hofsteter, 1984). Consideration is given to choosing hardware that will support the instructional strategies used in the CAI, provide adequate graphic design capabilities, and have adequate memory for record keeping and using authoring systems.

Software

Software is programs or electronic instructions that cause the computer to perform specified tasks. Systems software is programs that manage the resources of the computer, such as controlling the printer. These programs are written in a language that can give commands to the computer.

Courseware

Courseware is software used for instruction. The term *courseware* is often used synonymously with software, but has a more specific focus on the instructional objectives, instructional outcomes, and other support documentation about classroom use. Courseware may also include adjuncts such as student workbooks.

CAI AND INSTRUCTION

The computer is a master teacher because the CAI courseware designed by teachers can accomplish most instructional activities. These include diagnosing learning needs, presenting instruction, providing instructional enrichment, offering remedial assistance, and evaluating learning outcomes.

Diagnosing Learning Needs

CAI can be used to diagnose learning needs. Diagnosis can be accomplished before instruction by administering an entry test or pretest to establish the learners' current knowledge base and refer them to subsequent instruction. Diagnosis also occurs during instruction when the computer informs the learner of correct or incorrect responses and refers the learner for remediation or subsequent instruction based on the learners' readiness. Diagnosis can also occur after instruction. The computer can track the learners' progress throughout the lesson and identify problems, questions, or processes the learner did not understand.

Presenting Instruction

A major feature of CAI is the ability to present instruction. The instruction can encompass a lesson, a module or course, or even an entire curriculum. The entire instructional unit is self-contained as the learner uses the courseware.

Enriching Instruction

CAI can also be used to enrich instruction by providing supplemental information or by giving learners an opportunity to interact with or practice course content. Instruction can be individualized as enrichment courseware is designed for varying learner needs.

Remediating Instruction

When learners have difficulty understanding CAI instruction, the learner can return to the original instruction for relearning or, more appropriately, to other instruction with new examples that clarify and facilitate learning. CAI can also be designed for the remedial mode with other instruction, for example, to be used by students who did not understand a lecture presentation.

Evaluating Instruction

CAI is also used to evaluate learning outcomes. This is accomplished by testing incorporated in the courseware to measure outcomes after a CAI lesson. Evaluation using the computer can also occur after instruction has been presented using other media. In these instances CAI can be used for lesson or course examinations, challenge examinations, placement examinations, or review examinations for licensure or certification.

CAI INSTRUCTIONAL STRATEGIES

The computer lends itself to several instructional strategies. These include drill and practice, tutorial, simulation, gaming, problem solving, model building, and testing. Drill and practice, tutorial, simulation, and testing are the most common and are discussed in greater detail in Chapters 7, 8, 9, and 10.

Drill and Practice

Drill and practice exercises are a computer version of "flash cards" used for drill of previously learned facts or concepts. The drill and practice strategy is, therefore, used for enrichment or remediation rather than instruction or evaluation.

In CAI drill and practice a fact, term, or concept is presented and the learner identifies or chooses the correct definition. Feedback is given to the learner showing that the definition or problem solution was correct or incorrect and the next item is presented. The goal of drill and practice exercises is for the learner to obtain mastery of these items.

Drill and practice exercises can be used in basic education programs as well as for client instruction. They can be used by students to learn terminology, to memorize drugs, actions, and side effects, to master visual recognition skills such as ECG interpretation, or to practice math skills such as calculating drug doses or intravenous infusion rates. Drill and practice exercises are used effectively with the client to practice health risk factor identification, learn diet plans, or memorize side effects of medications.

Tutorial

The CAI tutorial is in effect a master teacher giving individualized instruction. Information is provided, the learner interacts with the instruction by answering questions, and then, depending on the response, is either given additional "tutoring" or progresses to the next unit of instruction. Tutorials are used for presenting instruction, enrichment, or remediation.

Tutorials are ideally suited for professional education and client instruction. They are used to present new content or to individualize instruction for learners with diverse learning needs. Because tutorials can be used as primary instruction they are often used for staff development or continuing education to provide an update about new procedures or knowledge. Tutorials can be used with clients to provide preoperative or postoperative instruction, or to teach clients about identifying health risk factors, managing their health problems or following a diet, or using prescribed medications.

Simulation

A simulation is a resemblance of a social or physical reality, a correspondence to a real-life situation that the student or client might encounter. The simulation strategy is used after the learner has mastered content because the learner is required to use higher cognitive skills of application and analysis or synthesis. Simulation is used for remediation, enrichment, or evaluation, rather than for basic instruction.

Simulations are a popular CAI strategy in the education of health care professionals because the learner can engage in clinical activities and decisions in a safe environment. The simulated activities of data gathering and interventions can be conducted without harm to a client or health care agency. Simulations can also be used with clients to provide an opportunity for making judgments about self-care.

Gaming

An instructional game is a goal-oriented activity that uses a set of rules that specify how a goal can be attained. The use of the rules creates a conflict that is rewarded by winning. Gaming can be used with drill and practice, tutorials, or simulations. It can introduce an element of competition with oneself or others in terms of time limits or points accumulated. The win element adds motivation to instruction that might otherwise be boring to the learner.

Games can also be used to teach cooperation instead of competition. In this instance, the game promotes use of affective skills, group problem solving, and teamwork. Learners typically work in small groups or teams in which each learner contributes to the problem's solution. Benefits of learning are also derived from the team interaction used to solve the problem posed by the CAI lesson.

Problem Solving

Problem solving focuses on the process or steps used to solve a problem. It requires the learner to combine rules learned from other teaching strategies to form higher order rules (more complex rules) for problem solution. In CAI problem-solving lessons, the learner generates the problems to be solved and uses or deduces appropriate problem-solving steps. Problem solving is used for enrichment, remediation, and evaluation.

Problem solving is used in professional education and client education to assist learners in learning steps of problem solution and in becoming aware of how they are solving problems. Problem-solving models such as the nursing process, medical diagnosis, or organizational management processes form the basis for this instructional strategy.

Model Building

Model building is a sophisticated and advanced strategy in which the learner constructs and tests models. Students create hypothetical situations in which the hypothesis, models, and theories can be tested.

Model building requires the learner to use synthesis and analysis skills. Model building is useful for conducting research and testing models and can also be used to learn strategic planning.

Testing

Computer assisted testing as an instructional strategy is used to evaluate the acquisition of knowledge, skills, or attitudes. This strategy is often used after drill and practice or tutorial to measure learning outcomes. CAI testing can also be used to administer achievement examinations, challenge examinations, or standardized tests such as state board examination reviews.

A testing system involves developing a bank of questions, designing the test based on objectives, and selecting questions to meet those objectives. The testing system also has the capabilities of administering the test, grading the test, and reporting results to students and teachers. The test items can also be analyzed for validity and reliability.

Testing is a common instructional strategy in education and in service or training settings. Tests are used to monitor learning outcomes and make judgments about learners' capabilities for safe practice. Tests can be incorporated in courseware or can constitute the entire CAI lesson.

ADVANTAGES AND DISADVANTAGES OF CAI

As with any medium of instruction there are advantages and disadvantages of CAI (Table 1-1). A careful consideration of these advantages and disadvantages provides the foundation for choosing and using the computer as a medium of instruction.

TABLE 1-1. ADVANTAGES AND DISADVANTAGES OF CAI

Advantages	Disadvantages
Individualized instruction	Development time
Quality instruction	Development cost
Time efficiency	Limited repertoire of instructional strategies
Effectiveness	
Replicability	Limited range of media features
Teaching–Learning principles well defined	Change in role of instructor
	Change in role of learner
Decision-making skills used by learner	
Mediation of instruction	
Interactivity	
Learner control	
Immediate feedback	
Improved attitude to content	
Privacy	
Accessibility	

Advantages

CAI has many advantages as documented by current research (Bangert-Downs, et al., 1984; Day & Payne, 1984; Huckaby, et al., 1979; Murphy, 1984; Payliaro, 1984). These include individualization of instruction, high-quality instruction, savings of instructional time, emphasis on teaching–learning, replicability, development of decision-making skills, mediation of instruction, interactivity, learner control, immediate feedback, improved attitude, privacy, and accessibility.

Individualized Instruction. One of the main advantages of CAI is the ability to adapt instruction for individual learners. Instruction can be designed to vary presentation, feedback, and remediation depending on the needs of a given student.

Individualized instruction is important when the variability of the learners is great. High achievers, for example, can quickly master instruction and move on to other more enriching instruction, whereas low achievers can spend as much time and receive remedial help as needed to meet learning objectives.

Quality Instruction. CAI courseware is preplanned and designed, using master teachers and content experts. All learners have an opportunity to benefit from this expertise.

In education of health care professionals the experts can be used to assure quality instructional experience. CAI can also be used to standardize instruction for continuing education units.

Time Efficiency and Effectiveness. CAI saves teaching and learning time. Once the lesson, module, course, or curriculum has been developed, the teaching time is negligible because learners use the courseware independently. Instructional time can now be used for interpersonal interaction with learners and for counseling.

When compared with other types of instruction (lectures, textbooks), CAI is as effective and more efficient. Some studies reveal that learning time can be decreased by as much as one-third (Bangert-Downs, et al., 1984). Other studies show that CAI is as effective as a lecture in presenting instruction but decreases instructional time (Day & Payne, 1984).

Replicability. CAI is a form of instruction that provides consistent instruction for all learners. Unlike lectures, demonstration, or clinical experience with a client, CAI lessons present the same instruction to each student and subsequent groups of students. Simulations, for example, can be used to provide the same clinical example for all students.

Emphasis on Teaching–Learning Principles. Well-designed CAI is based on current research about how individuals learn. Each lesson has defined instructional specifications with identified learning outcomes. Evaluation is an integral component of instruction and changes in learner behavior can be documented after CAI use.

Development of Decision-making Skills. Unlike lecture or textbook presentations of instruction, CAI lessons assist students to master decision-making and problem-solving skills. Safe environments in which learners can make choices or complete all steps of a process in a time-limited setting give learners the opportunity to explore alternative courses of action. Learners also discover effective solutions to problems and their own problem-solving style.

Mediation of Instruction. Another advantage of CAI is the ability to present instruction in a variety of ways to each student. CAI is a patient, consistent, and fair instructor with a wide range of instructional elements (activities used to facilitate learning). CAI can gain learners' attention, present objectives, provide stimuli, present instruction, give feedback, select learning sequences, give new examples, and evaluate instruction. This wide range of activities is indeed phenomenal for one medium of instruction.

Interactivity. CAI is an active form of learning. The learner must interact with the instruction by making choices and responding to feedback. Unlike lectures, textbooks, or passive movies or videotapes, CAI engages the learner in the instructional processes.

Learner Control. When using CAI the learner usually has control over the lessons. The learner can choose what to learn, how to learn, when to learn, how much to learn and how well to learn it, and how fast to learn. The advantage for the student is the ability to vary the pace and the time spent with the instructional material. These options are not available in lectures or continuing education workshops.

Immediate Feedback. CAI lessons have the potential for giving the learner immediate feedback as needed. The learner interacts with the content and is informed quickly that the response was correct (or incorrect). Rationale can also be included. Feedback given in CAI courseware is nonjudgmental and the learner is not embarrassed by making mistakes.

Attitude Improvement. A serendipitous finding about the advantages of CAI is that this medium of instruction improves attitudes toward the subject being presented (Bangert-Downs, et al., 1984). The improved attitude may be a result of confidence and competence with mastery of content.

Privacy. Learning (and mistakes) can occur in privacy when instruction is provided by the computer. There is decreased pressure from peers or instructors, and because students can take risks they are more likely to make mistakes and learn from the consequences.

Accessibility. CAI is becoming an accessible medium of instruction. As computers are located near learners, at universities, health care agencies, and at home more learners have access to quality instruction provided by CAI courseware. Locating CAI near the learner saves travel time and expense in attending a course or continuing education offerings (Parker, 1984).

Disadvantages

There are also disadvantages of CAI. Disadvantages include development time, cost, limited repertoire of instructional strategies, limited range of media features, as well as changes in the role of instructor and learner.

Development Time. The major disadvantage of CAI is the large amount of time needed to develop CAI courseware. Estimates are that 1 hour of CAI courseware requires 100 to 700 hours of development time. Unless a large number of users are anticipated and support teams and authoring aids are available, development time is prohibitive for many educators.

Development Costs. CAI is an expensive medium of instruction. In addition to courseware development the user must consider hardware purchases to support CAI use. If large numbers of students will use CAI, other costs are incurred in locating and equipping a computer learning station (Chap. 11). Although development costs are offset when training time, effectiveness, and safety are improved, the CAI author must weigh all costs against anticipated benefits.

Limited Repertoire of Instructional Strategies. CAI is best used for instruction in cognitive domains or in cognitive aspects of psychomotor skills. CAI has limited uses in affective instruction, although creative instructors are expanding uses in this domain.

Limited Range of Media Features. Depending on the type of hardware, CAI by itself does not use features of all media. Precise motion, lifelike graphics, and sound, for example, cannot be shown on most computers. Furthermore, CAI is difficult to curl up with in a chair and study! Information that the learner must read and review is therefore not suited for this medium. These deficits can be overcome, however, by adding adjuncts to the courseware.

Change in Role of Instructor. Using CAI changes the role of the instructor from teacher to instructional designer. In addition, much control and responsibility is given to the learner. These changes may cause discomfort for teachers who prefer interacting with learners in traditional classroom settings.

Change in Role of Learner. Use of CAI also changes the learner's role from passive recipient of instruction to active initiator. For some learners this change can cause anxiety and may require support for learners who are not self-motivated or self-disciplined.

THE FUTURE OF CAI

The computer and computer assisted instruction have been identified as the third wave of instruction (Ball & Hannah, 1984). Instruction was first transmitted by the spoken word, later by the printed word, and now in the information age by the computer. It is anticipated that as technology improves and costs decrease, the computer will transform methods and locations for teaching and learning. Educators must be prepared to maximize advances in instructional technology and interpret them for the needs of instructional health professionals and their clients.

Many are predicting that more learning will take place in the home and workplace (Naisbitt, 1982; Toffler, 1980). As costs of microcomputers and modems (devices used to link computers, usually through telephone lines) decrease, basic education, continuing education, and client instruction may occur in the home or at the health care agencies. The role of the educator must, therefore, change to that of instructional designer.

Scientific knowledge needed for safe practice is increasing rapidly. Health professionals no longer find themselves equipped with current practice skills within 1 year of graduation. New technologies for disseminating information are emerging to meet this need. Communication networks managed by computers, for example, already make this information available in the workplace. It is anticipated that these communication networks will grow as health professionals share data and knowledge bases. Again, health professional educators must be prepared to develop and use instruction communicated by computers.

CAI courseware development is in its infancy. Educators must become involved in developing courseware and using it in this medium of instruction in order to establish an instructional base for the future. You are invited to begin this adventure now.

SUMMARY

Computer assisted instruction is an effective instructional medium with increasing potential for use in education of health professionals, staff development, continuing education, and client instruction. CAI has capabilities of conducting a variety of instructional activities including diagnosis, instruction, enrichment, remediation, and evaluation. These activities can occur in seven instructional strategies: drill and practice, tutorial, simulation, gaming, problem solving, model building, and testing.

There are advantages as well as disadvantages of using the computer to deliver instruction. These should be considered when deciding to use CAI.

It is anticipated that CAI will be an integral component of instruction in the future. Educators must be prepared to create and use instruction for learners in the home and workplace as well as at colleges and universities and to adapt the improved technologies of instruction for education. Using and designing CAI provides the foundation for this preparation.

REFERENCES

Ball, M., & Hannah, K. (1984). *Using computers in nursing.* Reston, Va.: Reston.

Bangert-Downs, R., Kulik, J. A., & Kulik, C. C. (1984). The coming of age of educational technology: Meta analyses of outcome studies of computer-based instruction. In Proceedings of the 25th International ADCIS Conference, Courseware Transportality. Bellingham, Wash.: ADCIS.

Day, R., & Payne, L. (1984). Comparison of lecture presentation versus computer managed instruction. *Computers in Nursing, 2*(6), 236–240.

Fishman, D. (1984). Development and evaluation of a computer assisted video module for teaching cancer chemotherapy to nurses. *Computers in Nursing, 2*(2), 16–23.

Hessinger, L. (1981). Computer and videodisc: A new way to teach CPR. *Biomedical Communications, 9*(10), 12–13.

Hofstetter, F. T. (1984). Perspectives on a decade of computer based instruction, 1974–1984. *Journal of Computer-Based Instruction, 12*(1), 1–7.

Huckaby, L. M., Anderson, H., Holm, D. M., & Lee, J. (1979). Cognitive, affective, and transfer of learning consequences of computer assisted instruction. *Nursing Research, 28*(4), 228–233.

Murphy, M. (1984). Computer-based education in nursing, factors influencing its utilization. *Computers in Nursing, 2*(6), 218–223.

Naisbitt, J. (1982). *Megatrends.* New York: Warner Books.

Parker, J. (1984). A statewide computer interactive videodisc learning for Florida's CMS Nurses. *Computers in Nursing, 2*(2), 24–30.

Payliaro, L. (1983). CAI in pharmacology: Student academic performance and instructional interactions. *Journal of Computer-Based Instruction, 9*(4), 131–144.

Schwartz, M. (1984). An introduction to interactive video systems. *Computers in Nursing, 2*(2), 8–13.

Toffler, A. (1980). *The third wave.* New York: Morrow.

Additional Readings

Ahijevch, K., Boyle, K., & Burgen, K. (1985). Microcomputers enhance health fairs. *Journal of Nursing Education, 24*(1), 16–20.

Baker, F. (1978). *Computer managed instruction, theory and practice.* Englewood Cliffs, N.J.: Educational Technology Publications.

Bunderson, C. V. (1981). Courseware. In H. O'Neill (Ed.), *Computer-based instruction:* A state of the art assessment. New York: Academic Press.

Caldwell, R. (1981). Computer based medical education: New ways to meet persistent needs. *National Society for Performance and Instruction Journal,* December, 12–15.

Daynes, R. (1982). The videodisc interfacing primer. *Byte, 7*(6), 48–59.

Fisher, F. (1982). Computer-assisted education: What's not happening. *Journal of Computer-Based Instruction, 9*(1), 19–27.

Frye, B. (1982). A message from a computer: People programs and pac man. *Training and Development Journal, 36*(9), 84–89.

Godfrey, D., & Sterling, S. (1982). *The elements of CAI.* Reston, Va.: Reston.

Hassett, M. (1984). Computers and nursing education in the 1980s. *Nursing Outlook, 32*(1), 34–36.

Kirchhoff, K., & Holzemer, W. (1979). Student learning and a computer assisted instructional program. *Journal of Nursing Education, 18*(3), 22–30.

Lyons, C., Krasnowski, J., Greenstein, A., Maloney, D., & Tatarczuk, J. (1982). Interactive computerized patient education. *Heart and Lung, 11*(4), 340–341.

Mahr, D., & Kadner, K. (1984). Computer-aided instruction: Overview and relevance to nursing education. *Journal of Nursing Education, 23*(8), 366–368.

Manion, M. (1985). CAI modes of delivery and interaction: New perspectives for expanding applications. *Educational Technology, 25*(1), 25–28.

Mirin, S. (1981). The computer's place in nursing education. *Nursing and Health Care, 1*(11), 500–506.

Oliveri, P., & Sweeney, A. (1980). Evaluation of clinical learning by computer. *Nurse Educator, 5*(4), 26–31.

Papert, S. (1980). New cultures from new technologies. *Byte, 11,* 230–240.

Ronland, J. (1979). Computers and undergraduate nursing education: A report on an experimental introductory course. *Journal of Nursing Education, 18*(9), 4–9.

2

Selecting CAI Courseware

I. The Computer as a Medium of Instruction
   A. Instructional Intents
   B. Features of CAI
      1. Visual Representation
      2. Color
      3. Sound
      4. Motion
      5. Referability
II. Justifying the Use of the Computer for Instruction
   A. Users
   B. Time
   C. Content
   D. Money
   E. Access
   F. Acceptance
III. Locating Existing Courseware
   A. Publishers
   B. Reviews
   C. Clearinghouses
IV. Evaluating CAI Courseware
   A. Instructional Specifications
   B. Content
   C. Teaching–Learning Principles
   D. Instructional Strategy
   E. Lesson Design
   F. Screen Design
   G. Lesson Operation
   H. Documentation
      1. Teacher's Guide
      2. Student's Guide
      3. User's Guide
   I. Purchase Agreement
V. Evaluation Outcomes
VI. Purchasing vs. Designing Courseware
   A. Purchasing Courseware
   B. Designing Courseware
VII. Checklist: Selecting CAI Courseware

As CAI courseware becomes increasingly available, you will be making decisions about using and choosing CAI. The selection process requires an understanding of the computer as a medium of instruction and the ability to identify your own instructional intents and courseware requirements. After reading this chapter you will be able to describe the computer as a medium of instruction, to justify CAI use, to locate existing courseware, to evaluate courseware, and to determine when to purchase existing courseware or to design your own.

THE COMPUTER AS A MEDIUM OF INSTRUCTION

The computer is a vehicle for transmitting instruction, and as with other media such as videotapes, movies, lectures, or textbooks, it has advantages and disadvantages. To understand the computer as a medium of instruction you must have an understanding of your instructional intentions and recognize the features of the computer that will meet those needs.

Instructional Intents

Instructional intents are the requirements you have in mind for the content you wish to teach. These are usually written as purpose, goals, and objectives and are the vehicle by which the learning outcomes you have in mind for the learner are obtained.

In addition to identifying the instructional intents you will also identify the type of learning you have in mind. Learning occurs in three domains, the cognitive domain, or knowledge component, the affective domain, or the attitude and feeling component of instruction, and the psychomotor domain, or the skills. Although the computer can be used as a medium of instruction in all domains, it is most suited for instruction that occurs in the cognitive domain. At this point you should identify the domain in which your instruction occurs, and if the computer is not suited to this instruction, consider another medium of instruction.

Features of CAI

All media have features, or attributes, that facilitate instruction. These features include visual representation, color, sound, motion, and referability. Having identified the intents of instruction, you will be able to match your intents with the features of CAI.

Visual Representation. A large component of instruction requires visual representation. Some instruction can be represented by approximation and other instruction should be actual or lifelike. The computer is able to provide approximations of visual images using graphic designs. If your instruction requires realism, however, videotape, videodisk, slides, movies, or photographs may be more appropriate. You may also consider using these as adjuncts to your CAI.

Color. Color is used in instruction to highlight or contrast, or to represent reality. Color can be used (with a color monitor) with the computer to highlight and contrast. If your instruction requires actual representation in color, such as physical assessment of a client, photographs, videotape, videodisk, movies or actual clients are desirable.

Sound. The sound on most computers is limited to bells although recent technology permits access to high-quality audio. If your instruction is auditory, such as listening to heart sounds or taking a blood pressure, an audiotape could be added as an adjunct to the computer.

Motion. Skill demonstration and client responses to interventions use motion. Motion can be shown on the computer with rapidly changing screens, but if precise realism is needed, videotapes, videodisks, movies, or demonstrations may be preferred.

Referability. Some instruction requires the student to be able to refer back to the content, to read it again. Textbooks, lecture notes, and workbooks offer this opportunity. Although the learner can return to the computer as often as needed, the instruction presented by the computer should not be material the learner will need to access at a later time, such as notes for an examination, or laboratory values on a card that the student carries to the clinical setting.

JUSTIFYING THE USE OF THE COMPUTER FOR INSTRUCTION

Even though the computer may be an appropriate medium for instruction, use is expensive and must be justified to the learners, faculty, and administrators. The number of students, teaching–learning time, content of instruction, money, access, and acceptance of CAI as a medium of instruction are often considerations when making decisions about using computers for instruction.

Users

The use of computers is justified when there is a large number of users, such as a large class of students, groups of trainees, or clients who require extensive instruction. If the user group is not large, it is possible to redefine the purposes for which instruction is needed so that a greater number of individuals will make the purchase or development of courseware worthwhile.

Time

One of the main advantages of CAI is decreased learning time. Computer use is justified, therefore, when the time for instruction can be demonstrably decreased. Training programs and continuing education are two such instances when minimizing user-time supports CAI use.

Content

The instructional content also must be considered when justifying the use of the computer. Content that is stable and basic to a large group of students is preferable. Content that is in early stages of research or of interest to only a few, for example, does not lend itself easily for presentation by the computer.

Computer use is also justified when the content must be learned for mastery. Many cognitive and psychomotor skills must be learned for immediate application with clients and the computer is one medium of instruction that can facilitate this type of learning.

Another justification for computer use is content for which clinical applications are difficult to obtain or the risk of error is high. In these instances tutorials and simulations provide learners with opportunities that may otherwise be missing in the curriculum.

Money

CAI is an expensive medium of instruction and necessitates a commitment to purchase hardware as well as software, both of which may be expensive. Personnel must be available to maintain the equipment and manage a computer learning center. Money must be allocated at the outset for ongoing support of CAI.

Access

Learners must have access to the courseware. A plan for access must be established prior to purchasing (or designing) CAI courseware. Physical location, support staff, and storage facilities must be available in order to implement CAI use (Chap. 11).

Acceptance

Not all learners, faculty, and administrators accept CAI as an effective medium of instruction. Change tactics can be used to decrease resistance and promote support for change (Billings, 1984; Krampf & Robinson,

1984). Faculty and staff development programs may be needed to demonstrate how to use the computer and prepare faculty for role changes created by CAI. It is particularly important that faculty acceptance be obtained before selecting or designing CAI.

LOCATING EXISTING COURSEWARE

If you have determined that your instructional intents can be achieved by CAI and that computer use is justified, you can either purchase or design your courseware. The first step to either purchasing or designing courseware involves reviewing existing courseware using the same systematic approach used to select or develop other instructional media. There are several resources available to locate courseware that is already developed. These include publishers, reviews, and clearinghouses.

Publishers

Several major publishers are developing courseware for a variety of subjects and for a variety of target audiences including students, staff development, continuing education, and clients. The courseware is advertised in journals and in listings distributed by publishers. Some courseware is advertised by the same publishers who publish textbooks for health professionals. Publishers can be contacted through sales representatives and usually by tollfree numbers to marketing departments.

Reviews

Another way to locate existing courseware is by reading courseware reviews in professional and education journals. Several journals have published lists of courseware that has been developed or is in the process of being developed (Software Exchange, 1985; Worrell & Hodson, 1984). By reading these lists you may be able to determine if courseware exists for your content area. You may be able to identify strengths and weaknesses from the review and decide if you wish to preview the courseware.

Clearinghouses

Educational clearinghouses such as Educational Products Information Exchange (EPIE) compile and review courseware offerings. These publications can be purchased or located at libraries. Computer data banks of educational media are another resource for locating media and CAI courseware on a given topic. Computer searches can be conducted at most libraries.

EVALUATING CAI COURSEWARE

When courseware that has the potential for meeting your needs has been located it is imperative to preview it before making a purchase. The courseware should be previewed by the faculty who will use it in a course as well as by a potential learner.

A systematic approach to courseware evaluation is advised (Cohen, 1983; Hudgings & Meehan, 1984). A checklist facilitates an organized approach to review (one is included at the end of this chapter for your use). Narrative notes may also be used to supplement a checklist (Table 2-1).

One way to preview the courseware is to use a general-to-specific approach in two or more uses of the lesson. During the first use of the lesson you can obtain a general overview of the lesson and a reaction to it. In the same manner that you would leaf through a textbook that you are considering for adoption you can browse through the lesson. At this time you should note the date of publication and version of the lesson, the credentials of the authors, the computer systems needed to operate the lesson, the general content area, the target audience, and ease of operation.

TABLE 2-1. NARRATIVE FORM COURSEWARE PREVIEW

Part I—Overview
Title of courseware:
Date of publication:
   Version:
Authors:
Target audience:
Content area:
Computer system used:
   Peripheral equipment needed:
Ease of operation:
Part II—Evaluation
Instructional specifications:
Content:
Teaching–Learning principles:
Instructional strategy:
Lesson design:
   Instruction:
   Interaction:
   Feedback:
   Remediation:
Screen design:
Lesson operation:
Documentation:
Purchase agreement:

A detailed evaluation is conducted during second and even third uses of the lesson. At this time pay attention to the instructional specifications, content, use of teaching–learning principles, instructional strategy, lesson design, screen design, lesson operation, documentation, and purchase agreement.

Instructional Specifications

Each CAI lesson should specify the purpose, goals, and objectives of the instruction. These should be clearly identified for the instructor and the learner. Courseware should be appropriate for the learner (target audience) and developed to meet learning needs based on a task or concept analysis. Courseware that is not appropriate does not have identifiable purposes, goals, or objectives and contains content for which the learner has not attained prerequisite knowledge or skill, or, on the other hand, is too easy for the particular group of learners.

Content

The content is the essence of the instruction. Evaluate the content for accuracy; much content in the health field is soon out of date and the content of the lesson should reflect current practice. The content should be covered in appropriate depth and should build on previous learning. The content should be presented in a way that is free of racial, sexual, or ethnic stereotypes.

Teaching–Learning Principles

Quality courseware should be based on accepted teaching–learning principles. As you preview the lesson, note that the sequence of instruction is logical. Also consider the type and age of the learner; many CAI lessons are adapted from teaching principles that are effective for children but if your students are adults these same lessons may not be appropriate. Feedback in lessons should be designed to help the student learn the material. Also note that sufficient opportunity is given for interaction and practice and that the practice is meaningful.

Instructional Strategy

CAI courseware uses four main instructional strategies: tutorial, drill and practice, simulation, and testing. When previewing the lesson the strategy should be evident. Generally, only one strategy should be used in each lesson. If more than one strategy is used, such as a simulation after a tutorial, the strategy should be used to achieve higher-order objectives.

Some courseware available for purchase is advertised as being a simulation but in reality is simply a series of multiple-choice questions about a client situation. This becomes evident only after review of the entire lesson.

Lesson Design

Most lessons are designed to provide instruction, interaction, feedback, and remediation (if needed). During the second review of the lesson, be certain to isolate and comment on each of these aspects of lesson design.

Instruction is usually presented as teaching statements with examples. During evaluation note that the statements are clear and challenging to the learner. The examples should be ample to explain the fact or concept. Some lessons allow the learner to request more examples if needed to better understand the instruction. This is a positive feature of lesson design.

The interaction in the lesson is typically accomplished by a question that asks the learner to respond. High-quality instruction can be noted when the questions are thought provoking and occur at higher levels of cognition, such as analysis, synthesis, or evaluation. Interaction in some lessons is confined to pressing the enter key to continue or to respond to a yes or no question. The interaction should be dynamic. In some lessons the student provides a constructed response; during evaluation determine if your students can respond correctly in a reasonable number of attempts.

The response-handling capabilities of lessons vary. In well-constructed lessons the learner must enter the response before the answer is revealed. Judge the lesson on these aspects as well.

Feedback to the response is also a significant component of instruction. Feedback may not be necessary after every answer, particularly if the student can discern the correct response. When feedback is given it should be meaningful and give the learner information about the correct response and *why* the response is correct. Feedback can become tedious and dull; in well-designed lessons the feedback is engaging and motivating. Again, if the learner is an adult, the feedback should be written with respect for the learner and avoid silly comments.

Remediation is an integral component of drill and practice and of tutorial lessons in particular. As you go through the lesson, select incorrect responses and ask for help. Follow each remedial path to discover what type of responses the learner will find. In well-designed instruction the remediation is sensitive to why the learner did not master the objectives and has positive suggestions and new examples for learning the material. Watch the learner who is previewing the lesson with you to determine his or her reaction to remedial components in the lesson.

Screen Design

As you use the lesson, critique the screen design. Words and pictures should be placed on the screen for instructional purposes and with consideration for aesthetics and ease of reading the screen. The title and direction screens should get the learner into the lesson quickly. The learner should be informed of how to enter responses and change responses if needed. Help options should be available and, as you watch the learner who is with you go through the program, note how many times help options are needed.

The learner should be able to move the screens forward and backward at will and leave the lesson or go back to a certain part as needed. Lessons which control the movement of the screen for the learner are very frustrating for adults and unless they serve a purpose in the lesson should not be there.

Graphics should be used to support rather than to detract from the lesson. When graphics are used to show an anatomical part or motion, they should be accurate and the criterial elements easily discernible by the learner. The screen should not be cluttered and hard to read. Often graphics are added to entertain and you will need to decide to what extent this is of assistance to your learners.

Finally, the lesson should be well-written. Screen after screen of text is not a good use of the computer and the text on the screen should contribute to instructional effectiveness. The lesson should also be written at a level of interest appropriate for your learners and use terms with which they are familiar. Your student previewer can help you answer this question.

Lesson Operation

The lesson should operate smoothly and with no assistance from the instructor. Operating directions should be clear to the learner and not too long or too difficult to recall.

Go through the lesson following the optimal or correct sequence, answering all questions correctly. Next, return through the lesson and choose alternative courses. Each incorrect answer should be plausible and followed with meaningful feedback.

When the member of the target audience is using the lesson encourage him or her to run the lesson alone. The learner should be able to easily make selections of options and enter choices. Also, observe the learner to see if he or she is bored, frustrated, or lacking in confidence.

Documentation

The courseware should be accompanied by documentation or guides for use. A teacher's guide, a student's guide, and a user's guide (technical manual) should be available with each lesson.

Teacher's Guide. The teacher's guide is written to give information about lesson use. The guide should contain the purpose, goals, and objectives of each lesson. In some instances a graphic design or flow chart of the lesson is included. Entry tests, pretests and posttests may also be available in the teacher's guide (they may also be included in the courseware). The teacher's guide may also give suggestions for using the courseware, such as how to prepare the learners prior to the lesson and how to provide suggestions for follow-up activities after the lesson. Data from field testing should be available and can be used to predict courseware effectiveness with your own students.

Student's Guide. The student's guide is written to orient the student to the lesson and provide adjunct information or workbook space. The student's guide may or may not be included in the purchase price of the courseware. Be certain the student's guide provides all needed material and supports or supplements rather than duplicates the CAI lesson.

User's Guide. The user's guide or technical operations manual gives information about the hardware needed to support the courseware and installation instructions. Read this manual carefully and be certain you understand the instructions. Test the lesson on the computer on which you will be using the lesson to be certain the information pertains to your particular hardware.

Purchase Agreement

The preview information should contain a purchase agreement that indicates cost, the policy about duplicating diskettes, the discounts for buying multiple copies, and the inclusion of documentation and the number of student guides. As courseware is revised and updated old versions of lessons become obsolete. Inquire if the courseware publisher has an exchange policy or grants discounts for purchasing updated versions of the lesson.

It is imperative to thoroughly understand purchase agreements and how the courseware can be used. Be certain you have tried the lesson yourself and with a student using the equipment on which the lesson will be used.

EVALUATION OUTCOMES

There are three main reasons to evaluate courseware: to determine if the courseware meets your instructional needs, to convince someone to buy it, and to improve the product. Since the purchase of CAI courseware represents a considerable investment of money, evaluating courseware is time well spent.

Having identified your own needs for instruction and having reviewed the courseware, you should know where discrepancies exist and be able to make a decision about purchase. The courseware reviews should be kept in a central file where others may read them. You may also want to return to the review if your needs change and the courseware seems more suitable at a later time.

If the lesson does meet your needs you will be making a request for purchase. A well-documented courseware review will indicate the careful consideration you have given to identifying your needs and how the courseware will meet them. Administrators are generally more responsive to such an approach.

Another outcome of courseware review is improved courseware. Much is written about the poor quality of courseware currently available for purchase. Reviews that are shared with the author and publisher may contribute to defining the market and the need for better or different types of courseware.

PURCHASING VS. DESIGNING COURSEWARE

You are now at the point of deciding to purchase the courseware you have evaluated or deciding to design your own. Several guidelines can be given for making these decisions.

Purchasing Courseware

You can give strong consideration to purchasing courseware when good quality courseware exists. It will be ultimately less expensive to make the investment than to develop your own. Courseware should also be purchased (or other media considered) if there are no resources or expertise available for CAI development.

Designing Courseware

Courseware can be designed when resources of time, money, and qualified personnel are available. Here lessons can be individualized to a target audience. Currently, little courseware is available and development of good quality products is needed. You may be a likely CAI courseware author and design team member because of your expertise and experience with the target audience.

SUMMARY

Choosing CAI courseware for classroom use requires deliberate decisions. The educator must first identify instructional intents and match these to the features and capabilities of the computer as a medium of instruction. CAI is an expensive medium of instruction to develop or purchase; use is justified when there are sufficient numbers of users, learning time can be decreased, the content is not likely to change, the money is available to support and maintain the computer, the learner has adequate access to the computer, and when the commitment from the faculty and administration has been obtained. Having decided to use CAI, the choice remains to select or design courseware. Searches in publisher catalogues, journals, or clearinghouses help locate courseware for review.

Courseware should meet indentified instructional needs and preview is essential to determine if the courseware meets those needs. During a preview, attention is given to instructional specifications, content, teaching–learning principles, instructional strategy, lesson design, screen design, lesson operation, and documentation. A purchase agreement should accompany the courseware.

Systematic evaluation for selecting CAI courseware is used to determine suitability for purchase; a checklist is included at the end of this chapter for your use. The preview can be shared with administrators to support the request for purchase. Finally, courseware evaluation should be shared with the developers to enhance product improvement. If selection procedures reveal no courseware is available for your instructional needs you can then consider designing your own.

CHECKLIST: SELECTING CAI COURSEWARE

Computer is appropriate medium of instruction:

1. Instructional intents identified
   a. Purpose   _____
   b. Goals   _____
   c. Objectives   _____
   d. Domain of learning.   _____
2. Instruction requires:
   a. Visual representation   _____
   b. Color   _____
   c. Sound   _____
   d. Motion   _____
   e. Referability   _____

Computer use is justified:

1. Sufficient users   _____
2. Learning time limited   _____
3. Money available for hardware, learning station,
   maintenance   _____
4. Personnel available to use and maintain CAI   _____
5. Learners have access for use   _____
6. Users, faculty, administrators accept CAI as medium of
   instruction   _____
7. Existing courseware available   _____

Existing courseware appropriate for instructional intents:

1. Instructional specifications identified
   a. Purpose, goals, objectives evident to teacher and
      learner   _____
   b. Learner needs identified   _____
   c. Learning needs identified   _____
   d. Learning task identified   _____
2. Content
   a. Accurate   _____
   b. Matches objectives   _____
   c. Free of stereotypes   _____
3. Teaching–Learning principles
   a. Evident   _____
   b. Appropriately used   _____
4. Instructional strategy
   a. Specified   _____
   b. Appropriate for objectives   _____

5. Lesson design
   a. Design structure evident   _____
   b. Sequence logical   _____
6. Screen design
   a. Layout appropriate   _____
   b. Text well written   _____
   c. Help options used   _____
7. Lesson operation
   a. Lesson can be operated by learner without assis-
      tance   _____
   b. Instructional paths complete   _____
   c. Lesson operates in reasonable time   _____
8. Documentation accompanies courseware
   a. Teacher's guide explains lesson use   _____
   b. Student's guide gives necessary information to use
      lesson   _____
   c. User's guide can be followed to operate lesson   _____
9. Purchase agreement accompanies lesson   _____

REFERENCES

Billings, D. (1984). A model for evaluating computer assisted instruction. *Nursing Outlook, 32,* 50–53.

Cohen, V. (1983). Criteria for the evaluation of microcomputer software. *Educational Technology, 23*(1), 9–14.

Hudgings, C. & Meehan, N. (1984). Software evaluation for nursing educators. *Computers in Nursing, 2*(2), 35–37.

Krampf, S. & Robinson, S. (1984). Managing nurses' attitudes toward computers. *Nursing Management, 15*(7), 29–34.

Software Exchange. (1985). *Computers in Nursing, 3*(1), 33–51.

Worrell, P., & Hodson, K. (1984). Computer software directory for nurse educators. *Nurse Educator, 9*(2), 32–38.

Additional Readings

Geisert, P., & Futrell, M. (1984). Evaluating classroom microcomputer courseware. In Proceedings of the 25th International ADCIS Conference. Bellingham, Wash.: ADCIS, pp. 97–103.

Lathrop, A., & Goodson, B. (1983). *Courseware in the classroom, selecting, organizing and using educational software.* Menlo Park, Calif.: Addison-Wesley.

Roblyer, M. D. (1981). When is it "good courseware"? Problems in developing standards for microcomputer courseware. *Educational Technology, 2*(10), 47–54.

Roblyer, M. D. (1983). The case for and against teacher-developed microcomputer courseware. *Educational Technology, 23*(1), 14–17.

3

Principles of Teaching and Learning Used in Designing CAI Courseware

Current research about teaching and learning provides a foundation for designing CAI instruction. Findings in educational psychology, instructional design, and adult education are of particular interest to CAI authors. After reading this chapter you will be able to summarize three theories of instruction, identify learning outcomes, and use elements of instruction derived from principles of teaching and learning.

THEORIES OF INSTRUCTION

A variety of theories of instruction can be used to describe, explain, and predict how people learn. The theories of behaviorism, cognitivism, and adult education are of particular interest to CAI authors.

Behaviorism

Behavioral psychologists believe all behavior is learned. They identify events external to the learner that influence behavior and describe how behavior is shaped by modifying responses to these stimuli. According to behavioral theorists, learning takes place when a stimulus is presented and appropriate behavior is elicited. Consequences (which can be either rewards or punishments) are provided following responses to assure repetition of the desired behavior. The goal of instruction, therefore, is to present the optimal stimulus and provide consequences to encourage the desired response.

Instruction, according to the behaviorists, should be arranged to reinforce desirable behavior. Reinforcement is provided by shaping the learner's response in the direction of the appropriate behavior. Shaping is accomplished by giving rewards to successive approximations of the behavior, by prompting the learner to choose the desired response, and by cuing or focusing the learner's attention on the desired behavior (Fig. 3-1). For behaviorists, therefore, learning is obtained by *practice* and *feedback*.

Cognitivism

Cognitive learning theorists believe learning is an internal event in which information is encoded, stored, and later retrieved. Behavior is an outcome of cognition, the act of knowing or thinking. Learning, for the cognitivists, involves a modification of the internal representations of knowledge the learner already has. New information is anchored to past experience. The goal of instruction, then, is to assist the learner to assimilate and accommodate new information (Wildman, 1981). Emphasis is given to the sequence of instruction that relates new information to the learner's current cognitive structure. Learning is facilitated by the optimal *sequence* of the instruction and the lesson designs that activate *memory*.

Adult Learning

Adults have different learning needs and use different learning processes than children (Knowles, 1970; Meirhenry, 1982; Neher & Houser, 1982). Adults bring a variety of knowledge and experience to the learning set-

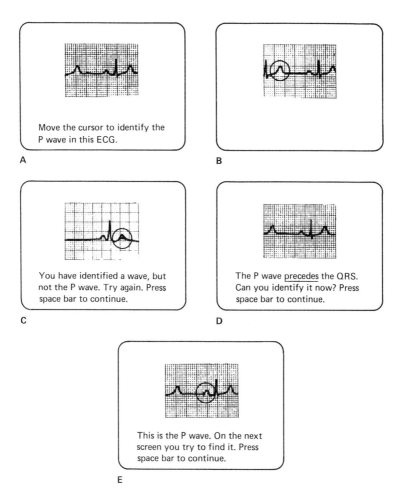

Figure 3-1. Shaping desired response. **A.** Question. **B.** Learner response. **C.** Rewarding successive approximation. **D.** Prompting. **E.** Cuing.

ting and consequently learning is unique for each learner. Learning is activated by the learner and is problem centered as opposed to content centered.

The goal of instruction for adults is to assist the learner to acquire information that is useful and relevant. The learning environment is modified to meet the special needs of the adult. Adult learners learn best when they can select the content and pace of instruction. Adults fear failure and the learning setting should be structured to tolerate mistakes and convey acceptance and respect. When designing instruction for adults, attention is given to allowing *learner control* and to creating a meaningful *sequence* for instruction as well as to enhancing *motivation*.

LEARNING OUTCOMES

Regardless of the theory used to understand the teaching–learning process, all instruction is designed to assure learner performance or learning outcomes. Learning outcomes have been described in several ways. One is to classify learning into domains: cognitive (knowledge), affective, (attitude, feeling), and psychomotor (skills). Objectives are written to guide the learner toward outcomes in each of these three areas.

Others have described learning outcomes by the expected performance in terms of what is to be learned: facts, concepts, principles, or procedures (Wedman & Stefanich, 1984). These cognitive activities are the building blocks of most instruction, particularly of the type that lends itself to CAI.

Gagné (1977) has also identified learning outcomes (Table 3-1). His list is expanded to include cognitive strategies, motor skills (psychomotor domain), and attitudes (affective domain).

All learning outcomes can be achieved by instructional strategies used with CAI (Table 3-2) (Gagné, et al., 1981). Facts, concepts, principles, and procedures, however, are the most common learning outcomes and must be determined prior to designing instruction.

ELEMENTS OF INSTRUCTION

The elements of instruction are the maneuvers or "moves" the teacher uses to facilitate learning (Table 3-3). Some authors have identified an extensive list of these elements (Fleming & Levie, 1982) which can be

TABLE 3-1. LEARNING OUTCOMES

Outcome	How Demonstrated
Verbal information	Recalling words, names, labels
Intellectual skills	
Discrimination	Differentiating 2 items
Concrete concept	Identifying by pointing
Defined concept	Identifying by telling
Rule	Identifying relationship of 2 or more concepts
Problem solving	Applying rules in new circumstances
Cognitive strategies	Demonstrating awareness of methods used to learn and solve problems
Motor skills	Performing psychomotor skills
Attitudes	Recognizing feelings, thoughts, attitudes

Adapted from Gagné, R. (1977). The conditions of learning. New York: Holt, Rinehart & Winston.

TABLE 3-2. LEARNING OUTCOMES AND CAI INSTRUCTIONAL STRATEGIES

Learning Outcome	Instructional Strategy			
	Drill Practice	Tutorial	Simulation	Testing
Verbal information	X	X		X
Discrimination	X	X		X
Concept (concrete, defined)	X	X		X
Rule	X	X		X
Problem solving			X	X
Cognitive strategy	X	X	X	X
Motor skills (cognitive component of)	X	X	X	X
Attitudes		X	X	X

TABLE 3-3. ELEMENTS OF INSTRUCTION

Establishing goals or incentives
Establishing set (frame of reference, advance organizer, introduction)
Presenting stimulus (information, directions)
Posing problems
Obtaining and directing attention
Explaining
Making distinctions and generalizations
Providing a model (demonstration)
Using questions
Obtaining responses (answer, opinion, feeling, observation)
Furnishing prompts
Controlling participation
Providing a fact, concept, principle, or procedure
Providing examples or non examples
Providing practice
Guiding thinking
Achieving/avoiding closure
Assessing attainments
Providing feedback
Employing rewards/punishments
Summarizing

From Fleming, M., & Levie, W. H. (1982). Guide to the message design syllabus and how to understand instructional media. Unpublished materials. Bloomington, Ind.: Indiana University.

used as needed to guide learning. Gagné (1977) on the other hand has narrowed the list, but insists that each event be included during instruction.

When designing CAI courseware it is important to select the elements of instruction that will facilitate learning for a given group of students. Of particular significance to CAI are the instructional elements of providing sequence, giving feedback, improving memory, providing interaction and practice, giving learner control, and enhancing motivation.

Providing Sequence

The sequence of instruction is the order in which instructional events occur. The sequence in computer assisted instruction typically involves presenting instruction, giving examples, encouraging interaction (usually with questions or problem-solving activities), eliciting a response, providing consequences (feedback), and following instruction with remediation, reviews, or progression to the next instruction. The sequence of instruction varies for each instructional strategy (Table 3–4).

The sequence of instruction should be apparent to the learner. It may be apparent by the structure of the lesson or it may be presented to the learner in a flowchart, graphic representation of the lesson, or other consistent overview.

Instruction. The instruction or instructional statement is the first part of any lesson. The instruction may be a fact, a concept, a principle or a procedure (Fig. 3–2).

TABLE 3-4. SEQUENCE OF INSTRUCTION FOR FOUR CAI
INSTRUCTIONAL STRATEGIES

Instructional Strategy *Sequence of Instruction*	Drill and Practice	Tutorial	Simulation	Tests
Instruction (Teaching statements)		X		
Examples (Examples, non examples)	X			
Questions (Interaction)	X	X	X	X
Learner response	X	X	X	X
Consequences/feedback	X	X	X	Depends on test
Remediation/progress	X	X	X	Depends on test

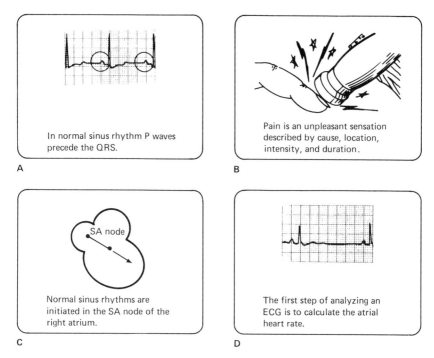

In normal sinus rhythm P waves precede the QRS.

A

Pain is an unpleasant sensation described by cause, location, intensity, and duration.

B

SA node

Normal sinus rhythms are initiated in the SA node of the right atrium.

C

The first step of analyzing an ECG is to calculate the atrial heart rate.

D

Figure 3-2. Instructional statements. **A.** Fact. **B.** Concept. **C.** Principle. **D.** Procedure.

If the content is new to the learner it should be presented in small units. Novice learners have difficulty comprehending the whole. Instruction should be based on previous experience and presented in a logical order. Easy to complex is one way; using the steps of a procedure or moving from general statements to explicit statements are others.

Examples. Examples are used to anchor new learning to old learning and make learning meaningful. Examples explain or demonstrate the concept being taught. There are several types of examples that can be used for explication (Fig. 3-3). "Close in" examples are very similar to the concept and contain most of the elements of the concept. "Far out" examples, on the other hand, are less similar to the concept but nonetheless include the range of examples for the concept.

Non examples demonstrate what the concept is not. Non examples are useful for providing contrast and clarifying instances that are potentially confusing to the learner (Fig. 3-4). As with examples, non examples can be "close in" (little difference from concept) or "far out" (wide variety from concept).

Both examples and non examples can be used to help the learner

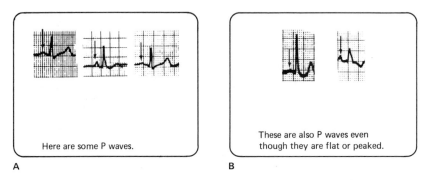

A   B

Figure 3-3. A. "Close in" examples. **B.** "Far out" examples.

differentiate the characteristics of the fact, concept, principle, or procedure (Fleming & Levie, 1978). When examples are used in instruction
it is advisable to use examples that are familiar to the learner first. Subsequent examples can be more complex and non examples are reserved
for last.

Examples can be used before or after presenting the instructional
statement or rule. Several guidelines can be used to decide when to use
the rule or example first.

The instructional statement or rule can be given first when the content is simple and all learners are familiar with the content. This type of
instruction is called RULEG (rule preceding example) (Fig. 3-5).

At other times it is advantageous to present the example first and
follow with the instruction or rule (EGRUL) (Fig. 3-6). Using examples
first can be used to present abstract or difficult concepts, but it is only
effective when the learner is familiar with the example. The rule can then
be discovered after several examples are given. In this instance it is best

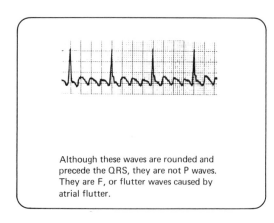

Figure 3-4. Non example.

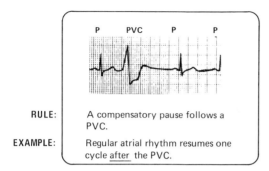

Figure 3-5. RULEG.

to give concrete ("close in") examples first and use more abstract ("far out") examples later.

Questions. Teaching questions (as opposed to testing questions) are used to facilitate interaction with the instruction (Fig. 3-7). Questions are used to stimulate recall of the instructional statement and to apply the knowledge in a new situation.

Teaching questions should be designed with care. Higher level questions (from learning taxonomies) facilitate greater recall of information. If the learner does not respond correctly at these higher levels, lower level questions can be asked until the learner is able to respond.

Consequences. Consequences are given when the learner responds to a question. Consequences (also known as feedback) can be informational or reinforcing (Fig. 3-8). *Informational* consequences tell the learner his or her response was correct or incorrect, and if incorrect why and what to do about it. *Reinforcing* consequences can be rewarding or punishing. Rewarding consequences are used to increase the likelihood the behavior

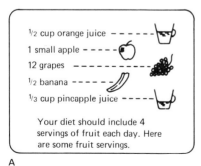

A

B

Figure 3-6. EGRUL. **A.** Example. **B.** Rule.

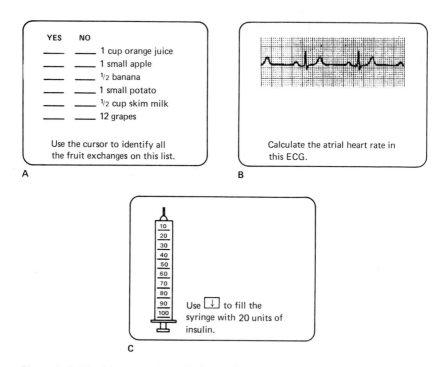

Figure 3-7. Teaching questions (**A, B** and **C**).

will occur again whereas punishing consequences are used to extinguish the behavior. Punishing consequences are not advisable in CAI as they do not facilitate learning. Instead, procedures such as shaping the undesired response toward a more acceptable one by coaching the learner toward the correct response can be used.

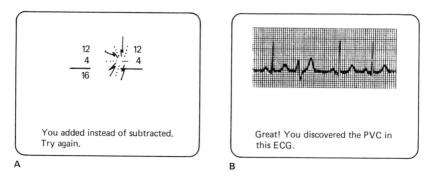

Figure 3-8. Consequences. **A.** Informational consequences. **B.** Reinforcing consequences.

Remediation or Progress. The last sequence of instruction is to direct the learner to subsequent instruction. If the learner does not understand the instruction he or she can be returned to a remedial lesson in which the instruction is presented again in another way, perhaps using different teaching statements and examples so the learner has an alternative way to learn the concept. If, on the other hand, the learner has mastered the content he or she can be directed either to enriching activities or to the next lesson.

Giving Feedback

Performance is improved when learners receive information about their responses. Feedback has a powerful influence on learning and is one of the most important elements of instruction used in CAI lessons.

Types of Feedback. As noted earlier, feedback is described as informational or reinforcing. *Informational* feedback simply lets learners know their response is correct or incorrect or, in the case of testing, that the response has been received. Informational feedback can also be used to help the learner locate the error and correct it, by directing the learner's attention to the process by which the answer was obtained as well as to the answer itself.

Reinforcing feedback, on the other hand, is used to strengthen the correct response or, if the response is incorrect, to coach or shape the learner toward the correct response. Reinforcing feedback can be external, given by the instructor (through the computer), or internal, the intrinsic satisfaction the learner has for knowing the answer was correct.

Timing of Feedback. Feedback can be given immediately after the response or delayed. Several principles can be used to determine when to give feedback.

Immediate feedback is given in new learning situations when the learner cannot discern the correct response. When learning new content the learner is easily frustrated and the motivation to learn decreases if feedback is delayed (Martin, 1973).

Immediate feedback is also supportive to low-achieving students. The feedback gives the learner confidence to continue or corrects misinformation before progressing through the lesson.

Immediate feedback should be given as soon after the error as possible. Then give the learner time to think about the feedback. A statement such as "proceed to the next section when you are ready" gives the learner an opportunity to reflect as needed.

Feedback can also be delayed, that is, given later in the lesson. *Delayed feedback* improves knowledge acquisition and retention (Cohen,

1985). Feedback is given at the end of the lesson when the learner is competent and mastery is the objective of the lesson. Delayed feedback is also appropriate when objectives are written for comprehension and application. Feedback at the end of a simulation, for example, facilitates learning.

Amount of Feedback. The amount of feedback provided to the learner can influence learning. The amount of feedback therefore must be considered in the design of instruction.

Feedback after every response can become boring and decrease motivation. Too much feedback can slow the pace when responses are correct and the leaner is confident. Feedback levels can be designed to be adjusted by the learner or given only for selected responses.

Ongoing feedback about lesson progress (advisement) helps the learner complete the lesson and attain mastery (Tenneyson & Buttry, 1980). Students who do not receive this type of feedback were found to quit the lesson before mastering the content.

Feedback can include the rationale for the correct or incorrect response. Learners may have guessed at the answer and, when appropriate, the rationale since a part of the feedback reinforces learning.

Feedback and the Learner. Feedback should be designed for the individual learner (Hartley & Lovell, 1984). Less feedback is needed for competent and mature learners. If the learner is familiar with the subject feedback can be delayed or given randomly instead of after each response.

Feedback and the Task. Feedback can also be adjusted to the type of learning task. Tasks in the lower levels of the cognitive domain such as those used in a drill and practice exercise should have feedback after every response. Learning tasks that involve problem solving on the other hand, can have feedback delayed. Feedback should also be delayed when the goal of instruction is to have the learner determine if the response was correct (internal reinforcement).

Feedback and Screen Design. Feedback should be interesting and varied but not distracting. Ringing bells, "smiley faces," and frequent use of superlatives has not been found to enhance learning (Friend & Milojovic, 1984). Feedback for the incorrect response should not be more interesting than for the correct response because the learner will select the incorrect response to see the graphics or the fascinating disastrous results.

Feedback can be personalized by using the learner's name. The learner can also be kept engaged with the feedback if a message appears on the screen while the computer searches for the feedback message.

The screen design can also facilitate feedback by showing the learner's incorrect response along with the correct response on the same screen (Fig. 3-9). In this instance the differences or relevant parts can be highlighted by the corrective feedback.

Improving Memory

Memory is the storage and organization of previous experience and retrieval when needed. Instruction is therefore designed to help the learner encode the message, commit it for storage, and recall it when needed (Bellezza, 1981). There are several teaching–learning principles that can be used to enhance memory.

Learning that is meaningful increases memory. Instructional statements can be written to give meaning to the learner. Advance organizers can be used at the beginning of the lesson to prepare the learner with what is already known and link it to what will be learned.

Practice also increases memory. The more time the learner can interact with the content the more likely the learner is to remember it. Knowledge and skills should therefore be practiced until they are automatic. Drill and practice exercises are an appropriate instructional strategy to improve memory.

Memory devices (mnemonics) such as words or rhymes can be used to establish a mental image. Other visual devices such as arrangement of words on the screen may also be of assistance to your learner.

Memory is enhanced when information is concrete. Familiar examples or diagrams help make information concrete for the learner (Fig. 3-10). As concrete information is established more abstract examples can be used.

Short-term memory is limited to about seven items at a time. Lists and diagrams on a screen should therefore contain no more than seven

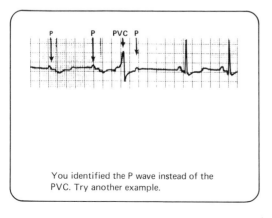

You identified the P wave instead of the PVC. Try another example.

Figure 3-9. Feedback and screen design.

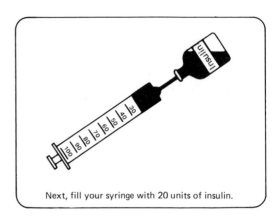

Next, fill your syringe with 20 units of insulin.

Figure 3-10. Facilitating memory visually.

items. The learner should have control of advancing the screen so as much time as needed to learn is available. If the learner will be required to remember complicated data (such as lab values, vital signs) this information can be presented off screen where it can be easily retrieved or the learner can be given paper and pencil to record significant data.

Memory is enhanced by varying the presentation format. Visual and auditory stimuli can supplement verbal stimuli to increase retention. Color and highlighting are useful in remembering criterial elements.

Providing Interaction and Practice

Interaction and practice enhance learning. People learn by doing and one of the major advantages of CAI is to give the learner unlimited opportunity for practice. Since much content must be learned for mastery, the elements of interaction and practice should be incorporated in each CAI lesson.

Learning is facilitated when the learner is an active participant. Active learning environments can be created for drill and practice lessons, tutorials, and simulations. In each of these instructional strategies the learner interacts by responding to questions and in drill and practice and tutorial lessons the learner has additional opportunity to practice as needed.

Practice that is short and frequent is preferable to one long session. Lessons should be designed to give learners several opportunities to learn content. Small modules or units of instruction (10 to 15 minutes) may be necessary for some learners.

Content that is being learned for the first time requires more practice. When presenting complex and new content it may be appropriate to follow the lesson with a drill and practice exercise.

Practice that occurs in a variety of contexts facilitates learning and application. You can, for example, present the content in a tutorial, have the learner practice in a drill and practice lesson, apply the content in a simulation, and ultimately practice the knowledge, skill, or attitude in a clinical setting. The variety of teaching strategies and learning settings facilitates knowledge, skill, or attitude acquisition.

Practice improves the learner's attitude about the content. The attitude may improve because the learner feels confident and competent and this may account for research findings of the positive effect of CAI on attitude toward content.

Facts and procedures require more practice than concepts or principles. When you are teaching facts and procedures it is important, therefore, to create opportunities for practice. Again, drill and practice is the instructional strategy to optimize practice with facts and procedures.

Giving Learner Control

Learner control refers to the ability of the learner to control the content and pace of instruction. There are several principles that can be used to guide the inclusion of learner control in CAI lessons.

Learners learn best when they can choose the method of presentation (Reigeluth, 1979). Some learners prefer learning the whole first and returning to understand the parts, while others learn from putting the parts together. Sophisticated instructional design systems can be used not only to give the learner control of the sequence of instruction but also to learn the cognitive strategy by which they learn best.

Learning time is decreased when the learner can determine the pace of instruction. Lessons can be designed to give learners options about what they need to learn, how they want to learn it (sequence), and how long they need to learn it. Using unit posttests, for example, will give the learner an opportunity to skip material already learned and move on to the next unit.

Learner control is also related to motivation. When learners can establish their own level of mastery they are more motivated to continue the lesson (Cox, 1982). When content is appropriate to give the learner control over mastery it is possible to design the lesson to give this choice to the learner.

Learner control is established in the lesson design by creating options for fast forward, review, and exit. It is generally advisable to at least give the learner an opportunity to quit the program at any time.

Enhancing Motivation

Motivation seeks to explain why some learners have greater interest and desire to learn and others do not. The computer as been heralded as a motivating medium of instruction and indeed some research has demonstrated that some learners are motivated by CAI. How can you keep your lessons motivating? Several principles can be offered to guide the development of motivating instruction.

Motivation may be related to attention span and learners lose interest when the pace is slow or blank screens appear while the computer searches for a response. Keep the pace moving or give the learner control over the rate of lesson progression. It is also useful to have a screen design or message appear when the computer is searching for information.

Some learners are motivated by the challenge of a game. All instructional strategies can be converted into a game by including a scoring mechanism or having the learner establish a target goal. Here the learner competes with himself. In other instances learners can be divided into teams (Chap. 11) and a game created by having teams compete for high scores.

Lessons lose their interest in 15 to 20 minutes. Lessons can be divided into modules or units so that no one section is too long. Interest can also be maintained by using several instructional strategies: in different lessons a drill and practice followed by a simulation, for example.

Graphics and illustrations can be used to maintain interest. Varied letter size, style, and color are two ways to make the screen interesting.

Motivation is heightened by curiosity and suspense. The sequence of a tutorial or simulation may be designed to keep the learners interested in the outcome or challenged by the responses they are asked to provide.

SUMMARY

Principles of teaching and learning drawn from behaviorism, cognitivism, and adult education are used to provide the foundation of instructional design for CAI lessons. The CAI author uses these principles to identify learning outcomes and select elements of instruction such as providing sequence, giving feedback, improving memory, providing for interaction and practice, giving learner control, and enhancing motivation to facilitate learning. A checklist follows to assist you with incorporating principles of teaching and learning in your CAI lessons.

CHECKLIST: USING TEACHING–LEARNING PRINCIPLES IN CAI COURSEWARE DESIGN

Providing sequence:
    1. Instructional events occur in a logical sequence   _____

  2. Sequence includes instruction, examples, questions, consequences, and remediation as needed   ____

  3. Sequence of instruction is based on learner's knowledge   ____

  4. Learner is informed of (or can deduce) sequence   ____

  5. Sequence progresses from simple to complex   ____

Giving feedback:

  1. Immediate feedback given when content is new to learner   ____

  2. Immediate feedback given when learner cannot determine correct response   ____

  3. Immediate feedback given to low achievers   ____

  4. Feedback given about process of determining response as well as the response   ____

  5. Feedback given soon after error is made   ____

  6. Immediate feedback given for objectives of recall and identify   ____

  7. Delayed feedback given for objectives of comprehend and apply   ____

  8. Time given for learner to think about feedback   ____

  9. Feedback is varied   ____

  10. Less feedback given to competent learners   ____

  11. Learners advised of progress in mastery lessons   ____

  12. Random feedback used when learner familiar with subject   ____

  13. Feedback delayed in problem-solving lessons   ____

  14. Feedback is individualized   ____

  15. Feedback is personalized using learner's name   ____

Improving memory:

  1. Advance organizers used to prepare learner for lesson   ____

  2. Memory aids used as appropriate   ____

  3. Examples are concrete   ____

  4. Graphics and diagrams designed for instructional purposes   ____

  5. Diagrams and screen designs have 7 or fewer items   ____

  6. A variety of stimuli used to support instruction   ____

Providing interaction and practice:

  1. Opportunities for practice are distributed over time   ____

  2. Lesson units are small   ____

  3. Frequent opportunities for practice are used with content unfamiliar to the learner   ____

  4. Opportunities to practice occur in a variety of ways   ____

  5. More practice designed for learning outcomes for facts and procedures   ____

Giving learner control:

1. Learner can choose objectives to learn (where appropriate) _____
2. Learner can choose sequence of instruction (where appropriate) _____
3. Learner can choose pace of instruction _____
4. Learner can choose mastery level (where appropriate) _____
5. Program designed for learner to move backward, forward, or exit the lesson _____

Enhancing motivation:

1. Graphics support instruction _____
2. Learner's curiosity aroused _____
3. Screen design is interesting and varied _____
4. Instructional strategies are varied from lesson to lesson _____
5. Lessons are 10 to 20 minutes in length _____
6. Incentives are established (goals, time limits, games) _____
7. Learner can control pace of instruction _____
8. Variety of stimuli used (verbal, visual, auditory) _____

REFERENCES

Bellezza, F. S. (1981). Mnemonic devices: Classification, characteristics and criteria. *Review of Educational Research, 51,* 247–275.

Cohen, V. B. (1985). A reexamination of feedback in computer-based instruction: Implications for instructional design. *Educational Technology, 25*(1), 33–37.

Cox, J. (1982). A new look at learner controlled instruction. *Training and Development Journal, 36*(3), 90–94.

Fleming, M., & Levie, H. (1978). *Instructional message design.* Englewood Cliffs, N.J.: Educational Technology Publications.

Fleming, M., & Levie, W. H. (1982). Guide to the message design syllabus and how to understand instructional media. Unpublished manuscript. Bloomington, Ind.: Indiana University.

Friend, J., & Milojovic, J. (1984). Designing interactions between students and computers. In D. Walker & R. Hess (Eds.), *Instructional Software: Principles and perspectives for design and use.* Belmont, Calif.: Wadsworth.

Gagné, R. (1977). *The conditions of learning* (3rd ed.). New York: Holt, Rinehart & Winston.

Gagné, R., Wager, W., & Rojas, A. (1981). Planning and authoring computer assisted instruction lessons. *Educational Technology, 21*(9), 17–26.

Hartley, J., & Lovell, K. (1984). The psychological principles underlying the design of computer-based instructional systems. In D. Walker & R. Hess (Eds.), *Instructional software: Principles and perspectives for design and use.* Belmont, Calif.: Wadsworth.

Knowles, M. (1970). *The modern practice of adult education, andragogy vs. pedagogy.* New York: Association Press.

Martin, J. (1973). *Design of man-computer dialogues.* Englewood Cliffs, N.J.: Prentice-Hall.

Meirhenry, W. C. (1982). Microcomputers and adult learning. *Training and Development Journal, 36*(12), 58–66.

Neher, W., & Houser, L. (1982). How computers can help adults overcome the fear of learning. *Training, 19*(2), 48–50.

Reigeluth, C. (1979). TICCIT to the future: Advances in instructional theory for CAI. *Journal of Computer-Based Instruction, 6*(2), 40–46.

Tennyson, R., & Buttry, T. (1980). Advisement and management strategies as design variables in computer-assisted instruction. *Educational Communications and Technology Journal, 28,* 169–176.

Wedman, J., & Stefanich, G. (1984). Guidelines for computer-based testing of student learning of concepts, principles and procedures. *Educational Technology, 24*(6), 23–28.

Wildman, T. (1981). Cognitive theory and the design of instruction. *Educational Technology, 21*(7), 14–20.

Additional Readings

Bovy, R. C. (1981). Successful instructional methods: A cognitive information processing approach. *Educational Communication and Technology Journal, 29,* 203–217.

Bunderson, C. V., Gibbons, A. S., Olsen, J. B., & Kearsley, G. P. (1981). Work models: Beyond instructional objectives. *Instructional Science, 10,* 205–215.

Glaser, R. (1982). Instructional psychology, past, present, and future. *American Psychologist 37,* 292–304.

Glover, J., Bruning, R., & Filbeck, R. (1983). *Educational psychology.* Boston: Little, Brown.

Gold, A. (1981). A technology of instruction based on developmental psychology. *Educational Technology, 21*(7), 6–13.

Jay, T. (1983). The cognitive approach to computer courseware design and evaluation. *Educational Technology, 23*(1), 22–26.

Malone, T. (1984). Toward a theory of intrinsically motivating instruction. In D. Walker & R. Hess (Eds.), *Instructional software: Principles and perspectives for design and use.* Belmont, Calif.: Wadsworth.

Reigeluth, C., & Darwazeh, A. (1982). The elaboration theory's procedure for designing instruction. *Journal of Instructional Development, 5*(3), 22–32.

Scandura, J. (1984). Cognitive instructional psychology: System requirements and research methodology. *Journal of Computer-Based Instruction, 11*(2), 32–41.

Sprague, G. (1981). Cognitive psychology and instructional development: Adopting a cognitive perspective for instructional design programs in higher education, *Educational Technology, 21*(2), 24–29.

Waldrop, P. (1984). Behavior reinforcement strategies for computer assisted instruction: Programming for success. *Educational Technology, 24*(10), 38–41.

Wildman, T., & Burton, J. (1981). Integrating learning theory with instructional design. *Journal of Instructional Development, 4*(3), 5–14.

4

Designing Computer Assisted Instruction

I. The Instructional Design Process
II. Product Formulation
   A. The Outline
   B. Resource Identification
      1. Time
      2. Money and Materials
      3. Personnel
   C. Time–Action Plan
III. Instructional Specifications
   A. Needs Analysis
   B. Learner Analysis
      1. Learner
      2. Knowledge
      3. Experience
      4. Problem-solving Skill
   C. Knowledge Analysis
      1. Task Analysis
      2. Concept Analysis
   D. Purpose, Goals, Objectives
      1. Purpose
      2. Goals
      3. Objectives
   E. Entry Tests, Pretests, Posttests
      1. Entry Tests
      2. Pretests
      3. Posttests
   F. Instructional Strategy
   G. Teaching–Learning Principles
IV. Product Design
   A. Blueprint
      1. Flowchart
      2. Storyboard
   B. Screen Design
   C. Writing the Lesson
V. Product Tryout, Revision, and Use
   A. Tryout

As the computer becomes a significant instructional tool, health professional educators with content expertise and experience with specific learner groups are becoming increasingly involved in designing instruction for this medium. These educators may be the sole author/designer/programmer of CAI courseware, or they may serve as a content expert or instructional designer on CAI design teams. Regardless of the role, the CAI author must be able to employ the various instructional design methods and procedures used to develop quality courseware. After reading this chapter you will be able to use an instructional design process and specific procedures to develop CAI courseware. You will also be able to describe the roles of five design team members.

THE INSTRUCTIONAL DESIGN PROCESS

Instructional design is a deliberate approach to developing instructional products such as lectures, videotapes, and tests, as well as CAI. The instructional design process involves identifying the needs for instruction, the learner, the task to be learned, the strategies used to achieve learning outcomes, and then developing instruction to meet those needs.

There are several advantages in using an instructional design approach to instructional development. One is that instruction is based on curriculum and learner needs. Furthermore, instruction is planned and purposeful with an emphasis on learning outcomes.

An instructional design model can be used to assure that each step of the instructional design process is followed. Although there are many instructional design models (Andrews & Goodson, 1980) an instructional product development model (Baker & Schutz, 1971; Billings, 1984; 1985) is useful for designing CAI. This four-stage model (Fig. 4–1) involves formulating the product, writing the instructional specifications, designing the course and trying, revising, and using the courseware. Interfaces occur in all stages. The model assures systematic design with an emphasis on product development; usable CAI courseware is the intended outcome.

PRODUCT FORMULATION

The first step of the model requires the author to formulate the product, to have an overview and plan of the courseware to be developed. At this time you will prepare an outline, identify the resources needed to produce the courseware, and develop a time–action plan.

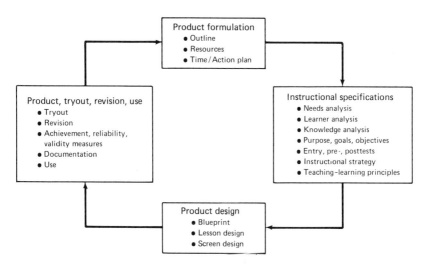

Figure 4–1. The instructional design process.

The Outline

An outline is an overview of the intended product. It includes the topic, the intended audience, the instructional strategy (drill and practice, tutorial, simulation, or test), a summary of the content, and if needed, the sequence of instruction (Table 4-1). The outline varies for each instructional strategy (Chapters 7, 8, 9, and 10) but should provide a consistent framework for product development.

Resource Identification

Since designing CAI courseware is expensive and time-consuming it is essential to identify the resources needed to implement your outline. During this preplanning stage, or front-end analysis, identify the time, money, materials, and personnel that will be needed.

Time. Developing CAI courseware takes time. Some estimate that 50 to 700 hours of development time are needed to produce 1 hour of CAI (Chambers & Sprecher, 1980; Garton, et al., 1984). Since it is your time that is involved it is important to allocate adequate time (and more!) to complete the project.

* Negotiate for release time from work.
* Be certain your time is viewed as important in the context of your job.

TABLE 4-1. PRODUCT OUTLINE

Topic:	Organizational structure
Audience:	Nursing students in leadership and management course First level staff nurses
Strategy:	Tutorial
Content Summary:	I. Components of organizations
	A. Purpose
	B. Philosophy
	C. Policies
	D. Procedures
	E. Job descriptions
	II. Patterns of organizations
	A. Formal, informal
	B. Centralized, decentralized
	III. Structure
	A. Division of labor
	B. Span of management
	C. Authority
	D. Communications
	E. Positions

- Be certain your employer understands the time commitment needed to produce quality courseware.

Unlike developing a lecture or preparing for a clinical conference or client education, designing CAI requires large chunks of time. When allocating time, specify periods of 4 to 8 hours for as long as needed to complete the project.

- Once you "get into" the design it is difficult to stop and pick it up again; allow for this phenomenon.
- At some points in courseware design it is crucial to continue forward progress; plan for this in the time–action plan.

Courseware can be more easily developed when a team approach is used. Here other colleagues and design experts collaborate to develop and complete the project. If you are working in a team environment, it will be important that time is available when all team members can meet.

- Establish group norms that promote free flowing exchange of ideas.
- Brainstorming with a design team during planning saves time in design stages. Work for consensuses on decisions.

Money and Materials. During the product formulation stage it is necessary to list all materials that will be needed for producing the CAI. These may include computers, adjunct equipment such as videotapes, or workbooks.

Other materials and equipment will be needed to design and code the lesson for the computer. Recently, software programs have been developed to facilitate designing and authoring courseware. These authoring tools may be used by the CAI author or by a computer programmer. Although the authoring tools decrease courseware production time, they are expensive and should be budgeted for during product formulation.

At this time it is also necessary to consider how the courseware will be used by the learners. Do you have sufficient numbers of computers? a faculty prepared and willing to use CAI? and space for the learners to use the courseware? Arrangements for these should be made during planning stages.

The money for CAI development and use must be allocated at this time. Have a clear understanding about availability of funds for equipment and personnel. You may need to submit a grant proposal to obtain development money, and the product formulation can serve as a basis for the proposal.

Personnel. Designing CAI courseware requires the expertise of a variety of people. Typically, a content expert, an instructional developer, and a programmer constitute a design team. You may fill one or more of these roles. If you do not, consider creative ways to find the needed support.

Ultimately, other people will be needed to manage courseware use. Depending on the extent of use, this may include other faculty, staff development coordinators, or client educators, computer maintenance staff, and learning resource center personnel. Planning for these now assures their availability later.

Time–Action Plan

Little is accomplished without a commitment for action. One useful approach to product development is to develop a time–action plan. Several planning tools such as Program Evaluation and Review Technique (PERT) or Critical Path Method (CPM) can be used and some are even written for computer use. One time–action plan lists the activities needed to be accomplished and arranges them in a logical order, establishes deadlines for each activity and assigns responsibility to a given person (Table 4–2).

Time must be allocated for each step of the design process. Although the time needed to design courseware depends on the type of courseware, the number of design team members, use of authoring tools and experience, a general guideline for estimating time for each stage of courseware development is given in Table 4–3.

INSTRUCTIONAL SPECIFICATIONS

When the overview of the product has been established and a commitment for resources made, the CAI author is ready to write the instructional specifications. Instructional specifications are statements of instructional intentions and include analyzing needs, learners, and knowledge, identifying the purpose, goals, and objectives, selecting an instructional strategy, defining learning outcomes, and using appropriate teaching learning principles. Each of these specifications is needed to insure the instructional effectiveness of the courseware.

Needs Analysis

A need is a situation in which something is required or wanted (Bell, 1978). The need may be perceived by the persons involved or ascribed by an observer. An educational need is one that can be met by a learning

TABLE 4-2. TIME-ACTION PLAN FOR DEVELOPING CAI COURSEWARE

Activity	Personnel	Week 1	2	3	4	5	6	7	8	9	10	11	12	13	14	15	16	17	18	19	20
Formulate product	Content expert	X	X																		
Write instructional specifications	Instructional designer		X	X																	
Design																					
1. Make blueprint	Content expert				X																
2. Design lesson structure	Instructional designer				X	X															
3. Design screen displays	Graphic artist					X	X	X													
Developmental testing	Content expert, Learners Language expert								X	X											
Revise simulation	Content expert, Instructional designer										X										
Try again	Content expert, Learners											X									
Revise	Content expert, Instructional designer												X								
Code program	Programmer													X	X						
Tryout	Learners, Content expert, Designer															X	X				
Revise/Debug	Instructional designer, Programmer																	X			
Achievement testing validity	Learners, Content expert, Instructional designer																		X	X	
Reliability testing																					
Write documentation	Content expert, Designer																		X	X	
Use	Learners, Faculty																				X

59

TABLE 4-3. ESTIMATING CAI COURSEWARE DEVELOPMENT TIME

Design Stage	Time Allocation
Product formulation	10%
Instructional specifications	10%
Product design	20%
Product tryout, revision, use	60%
Tryout, revision 1 (Developmental testing)	(20%)
Tryout, revision 2 (Pilot testing)	(20%)
Tryout, revision 3 (Field testing)	(10%)
Use, dissemination	(10%)

experience, and needs analysis is a systematic way of identifying these needs.

Educational needs arise from deficits in performance (skill), knowledge, or attitude. They reflect a performance gap in one of these areas. Needs can be identified by learners, instructors, or administrators and written as a statement of current results and desired results (Salisbury, 1984).

> Current: Average score on ECG final exam is 78%.
> Desired: Increase final exam average score to 95%.

It is valuable to develop CAI courseware for perceived or ascribed needs and later measure results of courseware use against these needs.

Learner Analysis

Learners differ in a variety of ways and it is important to have information about the learners (target audience) who will be using the courseware you are designing. Although learners (students, graduates, or clients) demonstrate the same variances as any group, particular attention is given to identifying the learners, their current knowledge, their experience, and their problem-solving skills.

Learner. Who is the intended learner for your courseware? Learners could be differentiated as clients, students, or graduates. If the learner is a client how old is he or she? Why is the person a client? Does the client have any motor–perceptual losses that make computer use different? What does the client expect to learn from your courseware?

If the learner is a student, is he or she an undergraduate or graduate student? Or a student in an orientation program or staff training program? What prerequisite courses has the student completed? What clinical experiences has the student had? In what courses is the student currently enrolled? Identifying learners in these ways relates the learner to learning settings and desired outcomes of instruction.

Finally, the learner may be a graduate in practice who is using CAI courseware for updating practice skills and knowledge. What background knowledge does the practitioner currently have? What are the knowledge needs? Has the learner used CAI courseware previously?

Knowledge. When assessing learners it is also important to determine their knowledge base. This can be done by reviewing curriculum materials or by giving an entry test that validates the learner's current knowledge. Since instruction is based on previous knowledge this component of learner analysis is crucial.

Experience. Learners differ with respect to clinical or practical experience. Clients, for example, do not have experience in giving insulin, some nursing students do, whereas most registered nurses have had much experience with insulin injection technique. Your instruction will be designed differently for each of these groups of learners.

Problem-solving Skill. Recent research indicates that learners use different problem-solving skills (cognitive models) (Benner, 1982; Larkin, et al., 1980). Novice learners obtain information in small bits and add one piece to the next to solve problems with careful forward progress. Experts, on the other hand, solve problems from a global perspective. They are able to assimilate and discard unnecessary data and focus on the problem to be solved. Instruction must be designed for these two different types of learners, and since CAI authors are experts and are likely to use global problem-solving skills, care must be given to designing instruction for novices.

Knowledge Analysis

When writing instructional specifications it is also necessary to identify the knowledge component of the topic or content you have selected for your courseware. The structure of the knowledge to be presented in the courseware can be analyzed to determine what to teach and in which order. The significance of knowledge analysis in the design of instruction must not be underestimated, for clear and meaningful instruction depends on selecting appropriate content for instruction. Two procedures will help you do this: one is task analysis, the other is concept analysis.

Task Analysis. A learning task is the behavior or skill necessary for performance. It is a concise statement of the operations or steps needed to accomplish an objective. Learning tasks may involve discrimination (knowing when to perform the task and knowing when the task is completed), problem solving, recall (knowing what to do and why), and manipulation (psychomotor skills).

An analysis should be performed when instruction involves procedures (interpreting an ECG, giving a medication, calculating a drug dose or infusion rate, performing range of motion exercises) or processes (making a diagnosis, teaching a client, developing a care plan, making a decision). Identifying the task and its component parts prior to instruction will encourage arranging instruction for efficient learning.

A task analysis is the procedure used to identify the learning task and its components and may be the most important instructional design procedure used to develop CAI courseware. Analysis moves experience and intuition often used as the basis of instruction to concrete and discernable steps that facilitate learning.

The procedure of task analysis involves five steps (Table 4–4). The first step is to state the main task. In this step you will make an overview statement of the task, such as: interpret an ECG. The next step involves identifying all the subtasks or substeps of the procedure or process. During this step you may simply list all of the steps that are involved, drawing on your experience or that of other experts or on policy or procedure manuals of a health care agency.

During the third step you will put the subtasks in a logical order, usually from first to last or in the order in which the steps should be performed. There is often more than one order in which tasks can be sequenced. The example given in Table 4–4, for instance, could be sequenced to have the learner identify the QRS complex in order to establish the site of origin of arrhythmias as the first step of the procedure.

The last two steps of task analysis relate the analysis to instruction. Here you will determine which steps of the procedure or process need instruction, and the degree of learning difficulty. To determine if the subtask requires instruction, you will need to be familiar with the intended learners and their knowledge and experience with the task. If, for example, none of your learners have had experience with the subtasks of identifying waves and complexes in an ECG you will need to provide instruction for each substep.

To complete the task analysis you should estimate the degree of learning difficulty for each subtask. Experience with the subject matter

TABLE 4-4. INSTRUCTIONAL TASK ANALYSIS

1. Main Task:
ECG Interpretation

2. Subtasks
Identify QRS
Measure QRS interval
Calculate ventricular rate
Describe ventricular rhythm
Identify P wave
Measure PR interval
Calculate atrial rate
Describe atrial rhythm
State interpretation

3. Ordered Subtasks	4. Instruction Needed	5. Learning Difficulty
A. Calculate rate 1) Determine normal 2) Determine abnormal	yes	easy
B. Calculate rhythm 1) Regular 2) Irregular 3) Regularly irregular	yes	easy
C. Identify P waves 1) Present 2) Upright 3) Precede QRS	yes	difficult
D. Identify QRS 1) Normal configuration 2) Abnormal configuration	yes	easy
E. Measure PR interval 1) Less than .20 sec. 2) More than .20 sec.	yes	moderate
F. Measure QRS interval 1) Less than .10 sec. 2) More than .10 sec.	yes	moderate
G. State interpretation	yes	difficult

and the learner will guide your estimation of learning difficulty. Learning difficulty tends to be associated with complex tasks, tasks that are unfamiliar to the learner, tasks for which clear examples are not readily available, and those tasks for which risk to client or errors of judgment are costly. Data from previous methods of teaching the content and results of examinations may also be a source for judging the potential learning difficulty. Subtasks that are identified as being difficult to learn require the use of additional examples and non examples as well as the opportunity for repeated practice. The task analysis procedure described above will give you this valuable information for lesson design.

Concept Analysis. Learning can also involve concepts, the set of characteristics or attributes shared by a group of examples. In order to teach concepts it is necessary to identify the concept and its attributes and to select examples and non examples that will facilitate learning.

There are several ways to analyze a concept. One simple way, familiar to most instructors, is the concept outline (Fig. 4–2). In the outline the concept is defined and headings are used to indicate the characteristics or attributes and their superordinate and subordinate relationships. Concept outlines facilitate making those difficult instructional decisions about what to include or exclude, how to show relationships of attributes, and how to sequence the instruction. A lesson on pain, for example, can be taught from several perspectives. In one lesson, pain can be presented as a subconcept of altered sensations with emphasis on descriptions of duration, location, and types (Fig. 4–2[A]). In another lesson the conceptual emphasis may be on differentiating acute and chronic pain (Fig. 4–2[B]). Here examples used in instruction would include instances of acute and chronic pain that include attributes of the source, onset, and course.

A more complex procedure is concept analysis. As with task analysis, this procedure involves steps which are performed in a sequential order (Table 4–5). The first step is to state the concept. Next the critical attributes are identified. These are the attributes which define or are essential to the understanding of the concept. When examples are used to explicate the concept, the examples must contain the critical attributes. The third step involves identifying the irrelevant attributes. The irrelevant attributes are those that are not essential to the definition of the concept and are used to decide which instructions about the concept are to be minimized, ignored, or used as less obvious or less necessary (far out) examples in instruction. The last step of concept analysis is to place the attributes in an order for instruction. Order may be from beginning to end, simple to complex, general to specific, or familiar to unfamiliar, or if the attributes are unrelated, a random order may be used.

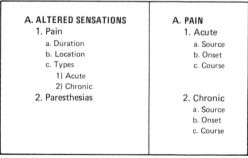

Figure 4-2. Concept outlines (**A** and **B**).

TABLE 4-5. INSTRUCTIONAL CONCEPT ANALYSIS

Concept:	Organizational structure of health care agencies
Critical Attributes:	Arrangement of personnel Division of labor Authority Management span Communications
Irrelevant Attributes:	Size, location, type of nursing delivery systems
Sequence:	Division of labor Arrangement of personnel Authority Management span Communications

Purpose, Goals, and Objectives

Having analyzed the need, the learner, and the instructional task or concept, you are now ready to state the purpose, goals, and objectives for your courseware. Since these are used by the learner to provide direction for learning, they are stated in terms of learner outcomes (Table 4-6).

Purpose. The purpose of the lesson is a statement about what the learner is expected to accomplish. Typical purposes of CAI are instruction, enrichment, remediation, or evaluation.

Goals. Goals are broad statements of how instruction will be accomplished. They give general direction to the lesson.

Objectives. Objectives are the specific learning outcomes for cognitive (knowledge) (Bloom, 1956), psychomotor (skill) (Harrow, 1972) or af-

TABLE 4-6. PURPOSE, GOALS, AND OBJECTIVES OF INSTRUCTION

Making Staff Assignments

Purpose: The purpose of this simulation is to give the student an understanding of the group process in the planning of care for clients.

Goals: To develop a cost effective quality nursing care assignment for a team of 10 patients.

Objectives: After participating in the simulation *"Making Staff Assignments"* the student will be able to:

1. Identify variables associated with planning staff assignments for small groups of patients.
2. Develop a staffing plan for a team of 10 patients.

Figure 4-3. Taxonomy of educational objectives.

fective (feelings) (Krathwohl, 1964) domains. Objectives have been classified according to learning outcomes in each domain (Fig. 4–3).

Objectives are written to include a subject (the learner), performance (observable action; what is to be accomplished), conditions (under what circumstances the performance is to occur), and criteria (to what specificity) (Table 4–7). Objectives give specific directions to the learner and serve as the criteria against which achievement is measured. Objectives are also used to guide the development of the lesson and are therefore well worth the time spent in writing them.

Entry Tests, Pretests, Posttests

Tests such as entry tests, pretests, or posttests can be used to assist the learner progress through lessons, modules, and courses. These tests serve as indicators of readiness for subsequent instruction and are developed for the instructional specifications previously identified.

Entry Tests. Entry tests are derived from the task or concept analysis and are used to ascertain the level in the task or concept at which the learner has attained mastery. They are administered prior to instruction to determine the learner's knowledge of prerequisites for the lesson. If learners do not pass the entry test at a prespecified level of mastery they are returned to other instruction that will prepare them for the lesson.

TABLE 4-7. PERFORMANCE OBJECTIVE

Objective:	Given a 6 second ECG strip the nurse will calculate the rate using the rule of 10 with 100% accuracy
Learner:	Nurse
Performance:	Calculate rate
Conditions:	Use 6 second ECG strip, use rule of 10
Criteria:	100%

Pretests. Pretests are used to measure the learner's knowledge (skill or attitude) about the lesson. If learners can pass the pretest at prespecified mastery levels they can be guided to more advanced instruction.

Posttests. Posttests are used to measure knowledge (skill, attitude) after instruction. They are parallel forms of the pretest and validate learning. When learners pass posttests they demonstrate readiness for subsequent instruction; if they do not pass the posttest they are referred for remedial instruction or advised to return to the lesson or an alternate form of the CAI lesson.

Instructional Strategy

The instructional strategy is a description of the final form of instruction and is determined after analyzing needs, learners, and knowledge. Drill and practice, tutorials, simulations, and tests are the most common CAI instructional strategies. Specific information about designing instruction for these strategies is given in subsequent chapters.

Teaching–Learning Principles

Courseware design is based on current research on teaching and learning. Principles are derived from theories in a variety of disciplines including adult education, educational psychology, and instructional development. CAI courseware development depends on the use of sequence, feedback, interaction and practice, learner control, memory, and motivation. Each should be included in lesson design as needed.

PRODUCT DESIGN

The instructional specifications provide a framework for courseware development. The next step of the instructional design process (Fig. 4–1) is to design the lesson (module, course, curriculum). Lesson design includes developing a blueprint, designing the screen and writing the lesson.

Blueprint

The blueprint is the overview of the master plan of the lesson. The blueprint is then used to code or translate the lesson to the computer. Flowcharts and storyboards are two tools used to develop a blueprint.

Flowchart. A flowchart is a graphic representation of the lesson, the structure of the lesson as it unfolds for the learner. Conventional symbols are used in a flowchart (Fig. 4–4).

Flowcharts are used to show the structure of the course or lesson. There are three main structures in CAI: sequence, choice, and repetition (Hord, 1984). The *sequence structure* is the linear progression through a lesson (Fig. 4–5). These structures are used in drill and practice and in parts of tutorials and simulations as the learner moves to another section of the lesson.

Choice structures are used to give the learner options (Fig. 4–6). The choices can occur before the lesson starts when learners select components of lessons to study or in the lesson as the learner chooses courses of action or responds to a multiple choice question.

The *repetition structure* is used to repeat a segment of the lesson (Fig. 4–7). This may occur in a tutorial or in drill and practice as the learner requests to review the instruction or to practice with the question and answer again.

- Use long sheets of paper to draw a flowchart. Used computer printouts make good scrap paper for this purpose.
- Trace out the instruction when the flow chart is completed to be certain all segments are included.

Storyboard. Storyboards, or screen maps, provide detailed development of the lesson by depicting individual designs for each screen display. They are similar to those used to produce a slide/tape or videotape program. A card, about 5 inches by 8 inches, can be used as a storyboard (Fig. 4–8). One side is used to design the screen and the other side is used to track screens that precede, follow, or to which the learner is referred in choice structures (Fig. 4–9).

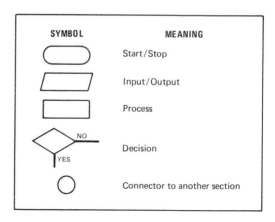

Figure 4-4. Flowchart symbols.

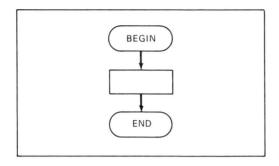

Figure 4-5. Lesson structure: sequence.

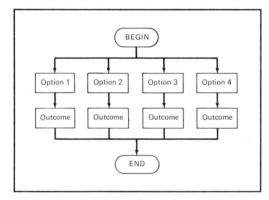

Figure 4-6. Lesson structure: choice.

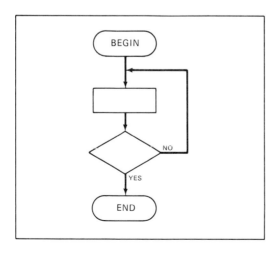

Figure 4-7. Lesson structure: repetition

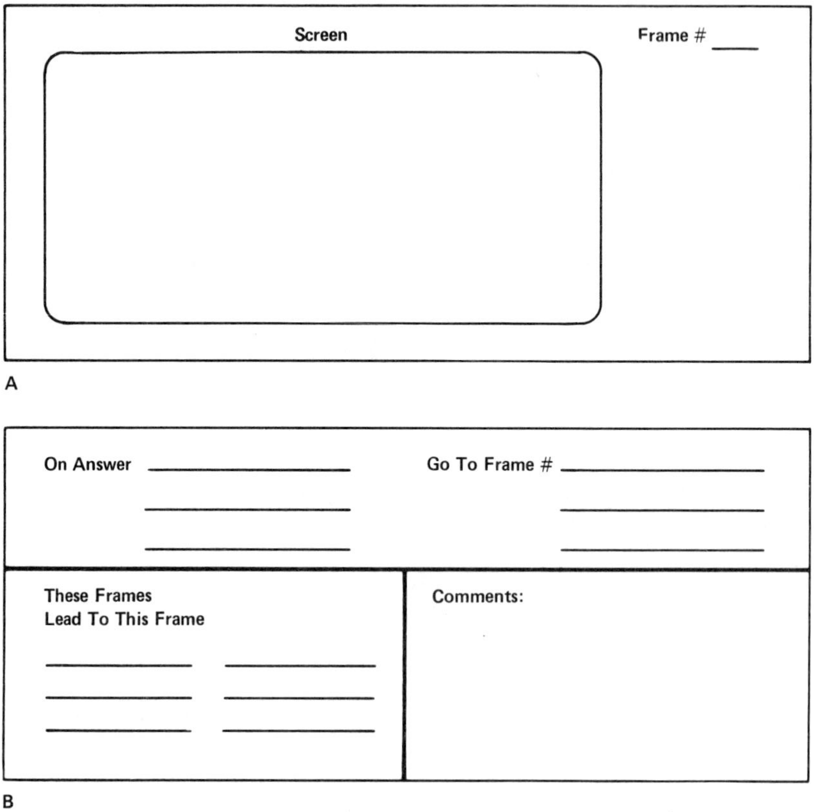

Screen   Frame # ____

A

On Answer _____   Go To Frame # _____
            _____   _____
            _____   _____

These Frames   Comments:
Lead To This Frame

_____   _____
_____   _____
_____   _____

B

Figure 4-8. Sample storyboard frame card. **A.** Front of card. **B.** Back of card. (From Orwig, G. *Creating computer programs for learning.* Reston, Va.: Reston, 1983, with permission.)

Once the lesson has been plotted out as a storyboard it is possible to edit the lesson and make any changes before it is committed to the computer. Again, it is possible to rearrange the sequence of the cards or redesign the screen before coding the lesson for the computer.

Screen Design

When designing the product and developing the storyboards, attention is given to the arrangement of text and graphics on the screen. The layout and graphic displays are sketched on the storyboard. A graphic artist is an asset to the design process at this stage of courseware development as color, type size, use of space, and animation decisions are made.

Writing the Lesson

Writing CAI lessons is different from writing textbooks or lectures. The writing style must be clear and concise. The text must also be visually attractive on the screen and unlike textbooks does not cover the entire screen. You should "rough out" the text on the storyboard to be certain your lesson text is as lean as possible and attractively arranged.

PRODUCT TRYOUT, REVISION, AND USE

In spite of your intense excitement to program and use your lesson now, you must resist and submit the lesson for tryout and revision first. Product tryout and revision procedures are more exacting in CAI than those used in other media because of the complexity of lesson structures. Removing errors before programming ultimately saves product development time.

Tryout

Product tryout involves at least three types of product testing: developmental testing, pilot testing (formative evaluation), and field testing (summative evaluation) (Arwady, 1983). The potential for revision occurs after each of these steps, and revision time must be allocated in your time–action plan.

Developmental Testing. Developmental testing is the first opportunity to try the program after it is designed. The blueprint is used as the basis for testing, and the more similar it is to the anticipated end product the easier it is to review. Developmental testing is done by a content expert, a language expert, and learners.

The content expert, or subject matter expert, is called upon to review the lesson for content accuracy. Many aspects of health care are controversial and your goal is to represent the best judgments of experts. Ask a colleague or a nationally recognized expert to review the lesson for its representation of current clinical practice.

The language expert is used to read the blueprint for syntax and clarity. A colleague from the English department or a friend with writing skills can be asked to serve as this expert. Typographical and usage errors are distracting to learners and should be corrected before the lesson is programmed.

Learners are also valuable experts during developmental testing. Ask two or three students to go through the lesson. Select these learners to represent high and low achievers or other variations in your target audience. Instruct the learner to go through the program and observe for problem areas. You will find where directions are unclear, connecting points are missing, sequence is out of order, and a variety of other problems students are likely to detect.

Pilot Testing. During developmental testing you undoubtedly obtained many useful suggestions which were incorporated in the first revision of your lesson. Now you are ready to try the revised draft with members of the target audience. It is even more helpful if you try it in the setting in which it will be used (i.e., individually, classroom, small groups).

Figure 4-9. Storyboard sequence for choice structure. **A.** Flowchart. **B.** Storyboard.

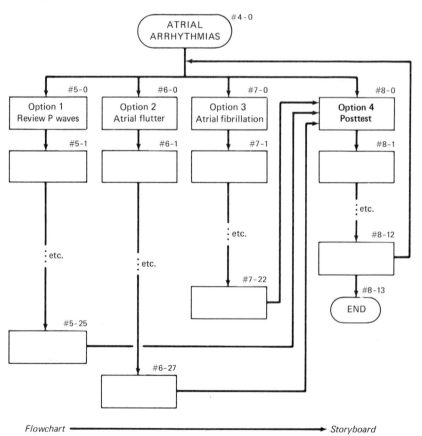

Flowchart ──────────────────────────────► *Storyboard*

A

Screen   Frame # 4-0

Atrial arrhythmias

Do you want to
1. review P waves?
2. learn about atrial flutter?
3. learn about atrial fibrillation?
4. take a posttest?

Move cursor to your choice

On Answer		Go To Frame #	
1		5-0	
2		6-0	
3		7-0	
4		8-0	

These Frames Lead To This Frame

1

2

3

Comments:

Opening screens precede

OPTION 4

Screen   Frame # 8-0

Atrial arrhythmias posttest

This test consists of 10 multiple choice questions. Choose the one
best response to each question. Your score will be displayed for
your information at the end of the test. If you do not answer
each question correctly return to the lesson for review.

On Answer	Go To Frame #
8-0	8-1

These Frames Lead To This Frame

4-0	7-22
5-25	
6-27	

Comments:

B

Achievement, Validity, and Reliability Measures

While you are using the lesson with the target audience you can obtain initial information about student achievement and lesson validity and reliability. Data from these measures provide useful information for subsequent revision as well as for documentation in the teacher's guide.

Achievement Tests. Posttests, unit examinations, or item tracking can be done to determine the number of students who respond correctly to each question. Test questions should be constructed so that 40 percent of the students can master 80 percent of the content.

In order to determine item difficulty you can make a grid to determine which questions can be answered correctly by most students (Fig. 4-10). The data for the grid come from an item analysis showing the percentage of students with correct responses to the question and the correlation coefficient of the correct response. The percentage of the students answering the question correctly is noted in the x axis of the grid and paired with the correlation coefficient of the correct answer in the y axis. Items of optimal difficulty are those for which 80 percent of the students answered correctly and have a correlation coefficient between 0.20 and 0.40. Questions falling outside of the optimal range should be rewritten.

Validity. Initial validity measures can also be obtained during pilot testing. Validity measures the extent to which the lesson represents the reality about which students are being tested. Validity measures answer the question, "Does the lesson provide instruction about what it says it does?" There are three types of validity: content validity, criterion validity, and construct validity. You can obtain measures for all three.

Content validity measures the extent to which the lesson is related

	ITEM CORRELATION	.40	.30-.39	.20-.29	0-.19	NEGATIVE	TOTAL
	VERY DIFFICULT 50%		/	/			2
	DIFFICULT 51-69%			////	//		6
Percent of students choosing correct response / difficulty	AVERAGE 70-80%	/HH/ /	/HH/ /	/HH/ //	/		20
	EASY 81-100%	///	//		/HH/ /HH/ /HH/	//	22
	TOTAL	9	9	12	18	2	50

Figure 4-10. Item difficulty grid. Darkened area indicates optimal difficulty level.

to content and answers the question, "Does the lesson accurately represent the skills, knowledge, and attitudes used in clinical practice?" Content validity of the lesson can be determined as the lesson is reviewed by the subject matter experts, colleagues (or if the lesson is for clients, other clients).

Criterion validity reflects the relationship of lesson score to other external measures such as clinical practice, course grades, grade point averages, state board scores, or certification examination scores. *Concurrent validity*, obtained from correlational studies, indicates the relationship of the outcomes of the lesson and the learner's current activity, such as clinical practice. Successful lesson completion correlates with safe clinical practice, for example. *Predictive validity*, on the other hand, correlates with other measures obtained on examinations administered some time after the learner uses the lesson, such as course examinations.

The third type of validity is *construct validity*. Here, performance on the CAI lesson is related to other learner variables such as job experience, learning style, grade point average, or intelligence. Correlational and factor analysis studies are conducted to demonstrate construct and validity and explain variances. Although not necessary to product testing, construct validity measures may be useful when examining instructional effectiveness.

Reliability. Reliability measures should also be obtained during pilot testing. Reliability refers to the extent that the learner's responses to the lesson and testing are dependable and predictable, that is, that the lesson will yield the same results with different groups of learners. Reliability measures are obtained by repeated use of the lesson. Limited reliability measures are obtained during pilot testing; other data are saved each time the courseware is used in order to substantiate reliability.

Field Testing. As a final product evaluation, field testing or summative evaluation is conducted after the lesson has been used by learners in other instructional settings or by subsequent groups of learners in the same setting. Again, validity and reliability measures should be obtained as well as information about lesson operation. Ideally, these data are shared with the courseware developer and the product can reenter the product development cycle for final revision, if needed.

Revision

The tryout and revision cycle is complete when errors have been removed from the lesson and as many people as possible have reviewed successive drafts. The final draft is used to code the lesson to the computer using a programming language or an authoring system. Of course, the final product once again enters the tryout and revision cycle, assuring error-free CAI courseware that can be used by the target audience.

Documentation

After final revisions have been made, manuals (documentation) are written for the teachers and learners who will use the courseware. Usually three types of documentation are needed: a teacher's guide, a learner's guide, and a user's guide.

Teacher's Guide. The teacher's guide is written to give the instructor information about the courseware. It can be written as a prospectus to give concise information for prospective users and can include title, content area, target audience, purpose, goals, objectives, the instructional strategy, and lesson designs. If entry tests, pretests, or posttests are used these may also be included in the teacher's guide.

The teacher's guide can also include information about using the courseware. Here you can share how the courseware has been used with your learners and give any suggestions to enhance use.

Learner's Guide. The learner's guide is developed to support the learner's progression through the lesson. Again, purpose, goals, and objectives are stated for the learner. Some lessons use adjunct written materials such as client chart information, care plans, or organizational charts. These are included in the learner's guide. Some learner's guides are written in a workbook format so students can refer to data gathered during the lesson.

User's Guide. The user's guide is the technical support manual for using the courseware. It explains the type of hardware needed to support the lesson and how to start the lesson. The user's guide also contains programming notes and design documents. Operation of learner management and record-keeping options (if present) are also explained. Finally, results of achievement testing and reliability and validity measures should also be included in this guide. The user's guide must be written to be read by instructors and learners who have no computer skills.

Use

The final step of the instructional design process is to use the courseware. After exacting development your lesson is finally ready to be shared with the learners.

THE INSTRUCTIONAL DESIGN TEAM

Developing a CAI product is a complex task as each of the steps of the instructional design process are followed. A team approach can be used to maximize efforts and use the expertise of several specialists. The design team can include the content expert, the instructional designer, the graphic artist, and consultants such as writers, test and measurement experts, and members of the target audience.

Content Expert

The content expert is the person who has the most knowledge about the content presented in the courseware. The content expert usually has experience with presenting the content to the learner and is aware of problems that learners incur when learning the content.

Instructional Designer

The instructional designer guides the product development process. He or she assists with writing instructional specifications, developing lesson structures, and with product tryout, revision, and use. The designer is knowledgeable about the medium of instruction and all aspects of CAI courseware development.

Programmer

Depending on the complexity of the lesson, programming languages or authoring systems are used to code the lesson for the computer. When programming languages are used, a computer programmer becomes a key member of the design team. Although this work does not begin until the lesson is designed, the programmer should be an active member of the team during all stages of product development.

Less complex lessons can be coded using an authoring system. Some content experts and instructional designers have learned to use these authoring systems, and since they are involved with product development at the outset they can easily translate instructional intents to the CAI lesson.

Artist

CAI is both a verbal and visual medium of instruction. A graphic artist lends expertise not only in designing the visual aspects of the lesson but also in planning screen layouts. Well-designed screens increase learner motivation and contribute to an attractive lesson. Adding an artist to your team can improve your lesson design.

Consultants

Others may be invited to join the design team at various stages of product development. During review stages, for example, other subject matter experts, the language expert, and the learner are invited to review the blueprint. When designing a test it is valuable to have materials reviewed by an expert in tests and measurements.

SUMMARY

Designing CAI courseware is a planned and deliberate effort. An instructional development model can be used to assure a systematic approach. A four-stage design process includes formulating the product, writing instructional specifications, designing the lesson (module, course, curriculum), and trying, revising, and using the final product. CAI courseware development is a time-consuming and detailed process; a team approach uses the expertise of content specialists, instructional designers, programmers, artists, and various consultants to ensure quality courseware development. A checklist is included at the end of this chapter which you can use as you plan, implement, and evaluate your own CAI courseware.

CHECKLIST: THE INSTRUCTIONAL DESIGN PROCESS

Product formulation:
1. Outline prepared   _____
2. Time allocated   _____
3. Funding sources identified   _____
4. Production materials available
     a. Computer   _____
     b. Authoring system   _____
5. User materials and personnel available
     a. Computer learning station   _____
     b. Prepared faculty and learners   _____
6. Design personnel identified
     a. Subject matter expert   _____

      b. Programmer   _____
      c. Instructional designer   _____
      d. Artist   _____
      e. Consultants   _____
  7. Time–action plan developed   _____

Instructional specifications:

  1. Needs analysis conducted   _____
  2. Learner analysis conducted   _____
  3. Knowledge analysis conducted   _____
  4. Purpose, goals, objectives written   _____
  5. Entry tests, pretests, posttests developed   _____
  6. Instructional strategy identified   _____
  7. Teaching–learning principles used in lesson   _____

Product design:

  1. Blueprint drawn
      a. Flowchart designed   _____
      b. Storyboard developed   _____
  2. Screen designs drawn
      a. Screen layout   _____
      b. Text display   _____
      c. Graphic art   _____
  3. Lesson text written   _____

Product tryout, revision, and use:

  1. Developmental testing, lesson reviewed by:
      a. Design team   _____
      b. Subject matter experts   _____
      c. Learners   _____
      d. Language experts   _____
      e. Other consultants as needed   _____
  2. Pilot testing, lesson revised and reviewed by:
      a. Design team   _____
      b. Learners   _____
  3. Achievement measures obtained   _____
  4. Validity established   _____
  5. Reliability established   _____
  6. Final revision; programming   _____
  7. Program tryout; revision   _____
  8. Documentation written
      a. Teacher's guide   _____
      b. Learner's guide   _____
      c. User's guide   _____
  9. Lesson used by target audience   _____

10. Other validity, reliability data obtained   _____
11. Summative evaluation   _____
12. Design team celebration!   _____

REFERENCES

Andrews, D. H., & Goodson, L. A. (1980). A comparative analysis of models of instructional design. *Journal of Instructional Design, 3*(4), 2–16.

Arwady, J. (1983). Field testing: A time for Alice and other real people. *Educational Technology, 23*(10), 32–34.

Baker, R., & Schutz, R. (Eds.). (1971). *Instructional product development.* New York: Van Nostrand Reinhold.

Bell, D. (1978). Assessing educational needs: Advantages and disadvantages of eigthteen techniques. *Nurse Educator, 3*(3), 15–21.

Benner, P. (1982). From novice to expert. *American Journal of Nursing, 82*(3), 402–407.

Billings, D. (1984). Computer assisted instruction courseware development: An instructional design approach. *Collegiate Microcomputer, 2*(1), 41–50.

Billings, D. (1985). An instructional design approach to developing CAI courseware. *Computers in Nursing, 3*(5), 217–223.

Bloom, B. S. (Ed.). (1956). *Taxonomy of educational objectives. Handbook I: Cognitive domain.* New York: D. McKay.

Chambers, J., & Sprecher, J. (1980). Computer assisted instruction: Current trends and critical issues. *Communications of the Association for Computing Machinery, 23*(6), 332–342.

Garton, R., Reed, M., Reed, G. & Stevens, E. (1984). Developing a CBI course: In the process. In Proceedings of the 25th International ADCIS Conference. Bellingham, Wash.: Western Washington University.

Golas, K. (1983). The formative evaluation of computer assisted instruction. *Educational Technology, 23*(1), 26–28.

Harrow, A. (1972). A taxonomy of the psychomotor domain. New York: D. McKay.

Hord, E. (1984). Guidelines for designing computer assisted instruction. *Instructional Innovator,* 19–23.

Krathwohl, D. (1964). *Taxonomy of educational objectives. Handbook II: Affective domain.* New York: D. McKay.

Larkin, J., McDermott, J., Simon, D. P., & Simon, H. A. (1980). Expert and novice performance in solving physics problems. *Science, 208,* 1335–1342.

Salisbury, D. (1984). How to decide when and where to use microcomputers for instruction. *Educational Technology, 3,* 22–24.

Additional Readings

Arenson, M. (1981). A model for systematic revision of computer-based instruction materials in music theory. *Journal of Computer-Based Instruction, 7*(3), 78–83.

Ball, M., & Hannah, K. (1984). *Using computers in nursing.* Reston, Va.: Reston.

Bell, M. (1981). A systematic instructional design strategy derived from information processing theory. *Educational Technology, 21*(3), 32–35.

Bork, A. (1984). Producing computer based learning material at the educational technology center. *Journal of Computer-Based Instruction, 11*(3), 78–81.

Bork, A. (1984). Production systems for computer based learning. In D. Walker & R. Hess (Eds.). *Instructional software: Principles and perspectives for design and use.* Belmont, Calif.: Wadsworth.

Briggs, L., & Wager, W. (1981). *Handbook of procedures for the design of instruction.* Englewood Cliffs, N.J.: Educational Technology Publications.

Burke, R. (1982). *CAI Sourcebook.* Englewood Cliffs, N.J.: Prentice-Hall.

Dick, W., & Carey, L. (1978). *The systematic designs of instruction.* Glenview, Ill.: Scott, Foresman & Co.

Gagné, R., Wager, W., & Rojas, A. (1981). Planning and authoring computer-assisted instruction lessons. *Educational Technology, 21*(9), 17–21.

Grobe, S. (1984). Computer assisted instruction: An alternative. *Computers in Nursing, 2*(3), 92–97.

Heines, J. (1985). Interactive means active, learner involvement in CBI. *Data Training, 4*(4), 48–53.

Kashka, M., & Lease, B. (1984). A design for the development of a computer assisted instruction tutorial model. *Computers in Nursing, 2*(4), 136–142.

Montague, W., Wulbeck, W., & Ellis, J. (1983). Quality CBI depends on instructional design and quality implementation. *Journal of Computer-Based Instruction, 10*(3 & 4), 90–93.

Morris, J. (1984). Documenting computer-based systems for industrial training. *Educational Technology, 24*(6), 15–18.

Orwig, G. (1983). *Creating computer programs for learning: A guide for trainers, parents and teachers.* Reston, Va.: Reston.

Peters, H., & Johnson, J. (1978). *Author's guide.* Iowa City, Iowa: Conduit.

Roblyer, M. D. (1983). Toward more effective microcomputer courseware through application of systematic instructional design methods. *AEDS Journal, 17*(1 & 2), 23–32.

Rosenberg, M. (1982). The ABCs of ISD* (*Instructional Systems Design). *Training and Development Journal, 36*(9), 44–50.

Smith, P., & Boyce, B. (1984). Instructional design considerations in the development of computer assisted instruction. *Educational Technology, 24*(7), 5–11.

Sprecher, J., & Chambers, J. (1980). Computer assisted instruction: Factors affecting courseware development. *Journal of Computer-Based Instruction, 7*(2), 47–57.

Swirsky, R. (1982). The art of flowcharting. *Popular Computing, 9,* 75–77.

5

Screen Design

I. Screens
  A. Configuration
  B. Resolution
  C. Advance Control
II. Screen Commands
  A. Menu
    1. Course Menu
    2. Lesson Menu
  B. Prompt
  C. Error Messages
  D. Editing
III. Types of Screens
  A. Title Screen
  B. Opening Screen
  C. Direction Screen
  D. Test Screen
  E. Lesson Screen
  F. Termination Screen
IV. Screen Layout
  A. Orienting Information
  B. Directions
  C. Lesson Text
  D. Response/Feedback
  E. Error Messages
  F. Options
V. Special Techniques
  A. Inverse Video
  B. Foreground/Background
  C. Underline
  D. Highlights
  E. Blinking/Flashing
  F. Graphics
  G. Movement
  H. Color
  I. Space
  J. Overlay
VI. Writing Style
VII. Checklist: Screen Design

The design of each screen display in the CAI lesson is an integral component of creating CAI and one of concern to all design team members. The flowcharts and storyboards that were written earlier form the bases for screen design and are now, depending on the coding or authoring system used, translated into screen designs. In this chapter you will learn about screens, screen commands, types of screens, screen layout, special techniques used in screen design, and writing style used in CAI lessons. After reading this chapter you will be able to design or make suggestions for the screen displays for your CAI lesson.

SCREENS

Screens, or frames, are the displays that appear on the CRT. They are what the learner will see when he or she uses your lessons and are described by their configuration, resolution, and advance controls.

Configuration

Screens can be imagined as graph paper or a matrix of rows and columns. The size of the screen matrix depends on the computer; typical matrices are 24 × 40, 24 × 80, or 192 × 280 (Fig. 5-1). The screen configuration therefore determines the dimensions of your lesson's screen.

- If you are using a typewriter to plan lesson screen designs you can set the margins to correspond to the dimension of your screen.
- The storyboard can be drawn to reflect the proportions of your screen.

Resolution

The screen is divided into dots of light or *pic*ture *el*ements known as *pixels*. More pixels give greater resolution or better picture quality. Low resolution screens contain 256 × 256 pixels that result in coarse, grainy screen pictures. Greater detail can be obtained with higher resolution screens that have 1024 × 1024 pixels. The amount of resolution needed depends on the detail of the artwork in your lesson (Fig. 5-2).

- Graph paper corresponding to pixels can be used to plot graphic displays in your lesson.
- Higher resolution requires greater system memory; consideration should be given to need for resolution and hardware configuration before designing the lesson.

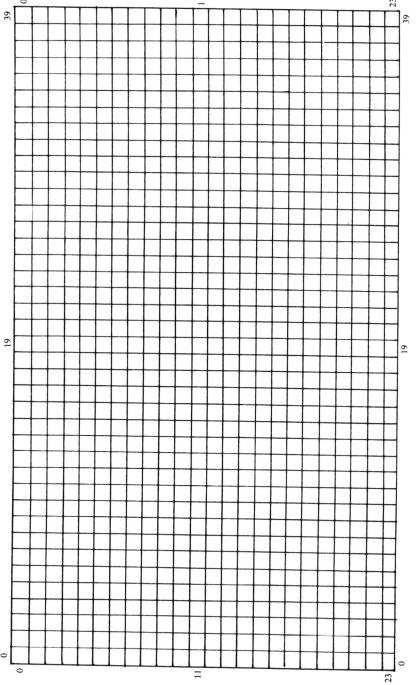

Figure 5-1. Screen matrix.

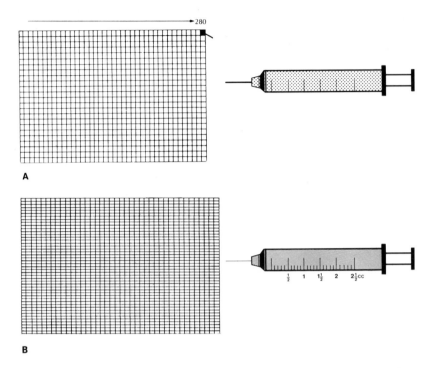

Figure 5-2. The difference in detail of high and low resolution screens. **A.** Low resolution. **B.** High resolution.

Advance Control

The screen can move forward (down) or backward (up). User control of the movement of the screen is known as advance control. Movement of one screen to the next is referred to as *paging;* continuous movement is known as *scrolling.* When designing the screen for your lesson you can determine if the screen should page or scroll. Scrolling is used to increase the speed of reading the screen but is generally not used for adult learners.

- Advance control commands should be written in a consistent form and displayed at the same place on the screen, usually at the bottom of the screen.

SCREEN COMMANDS

Screen commands are messages (instructions or prompts) used to help the computer communicate with the learner. Well-designed screen commands can guide the novice computer users through a lesson without their knowing much about the computer. Commonly used screen commands are menus, prompts, error messages, and editing capabilities.

Menu

A menu is a list of choices from which the learner can make selections. Each menu has a title, option list, and entry prompt (Fig. 5-3). Menus are used as overviews to the course and within the lesson to guide progress.

Course Menu. Course menus orient the learner to the course module or lesson (Fig. 5-4). They show the overview and sequence. As the learner progresses through the course the menu can be displayed to show the relationship of the current lesson to previous and future lessons.

Lesson Menu. Lesson menus are more subtle than course menus and the learner is generally not aware of using a menu. A multiple choice question, for example, is really a menu. Asking the learner to place the cursor on the right atrium in a diagram of the heart is another example of the use of the menu to present choices.

Lesson menus can lead the learner to submenus. Tutorials and simulations use menus in this way since the choice of one course of action leads to subsequent choices.

Prompt

A prompt is used to inform the learner what action to pursue. The prompt, "Enter your name: First name, Last name" tells the learner what to do (enter name) and how (first name first, using a capital letter for the first letter and last name last, with a capital letter for the first letter).

Prompts can be designed to be fully apparent or suppressed. When prompts are suppressed the learner can proceed more quickly through

TITLE: ECG waves and complexes

OPTION: Which ECG wave or complex do you
           want to study now?

           1. P waves
           2. PR interval
           3. QRS complex
           4. T waves
           5. Quit

PROMPT: Enter the number of your choice _____

Figure 5-3. Parts of a menu.

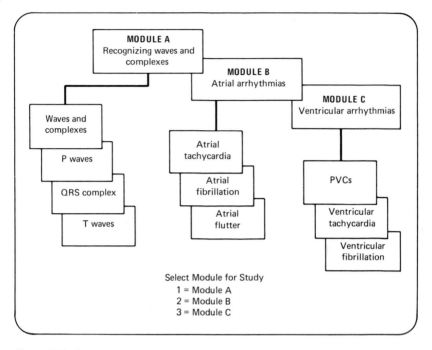

Figure 5-4. Course menu.

the lesson. In other instances you may wish to have the prompt displayed at all times.

- Observe members of the target audience who are helping you test the first draft of your lesson to obtain ideas where additional prompts may be needed.

Error Messages

If learners make errors in following directions or entering data you can inform them of the error and how to correct it (Fig. 5–5). Error messages can be designed to appear automatically or at the request of the learner, or a combination of both. Error messages are used for mistakes related to computer use, not content errors.

- Avoid silly or denigrating error messages, such as "Wrong again, dummy."

Editing

Edit refers to the capability of the learner to correct an error, change an answer, or enter additional information. In tests and tutorials it is important for you to design your lesson to include editing capabilities. Ex-

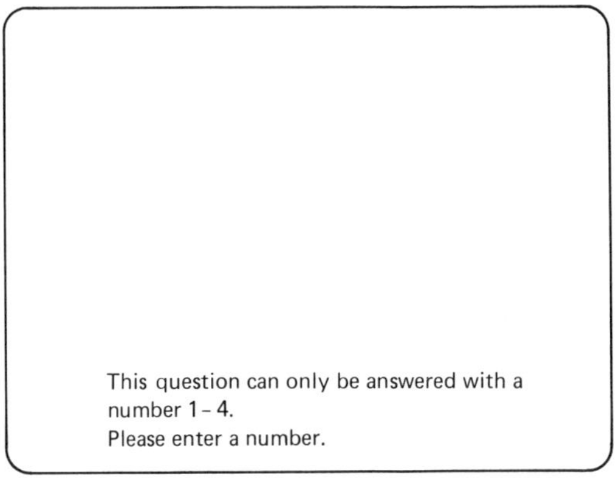

This question can only be answered with a
number 1 - 4.
Please enter a number.

Figure 5-5. Error message.

amples of edit prompts are: "Is this the answer you want to enter?",
"Are you certain your answer is correct?", "Do you wish to change any
answers before you complete this test?"

Editing capabilities used during a test can increase the learner's anxiety by casting doubts about the answer. Use editing consistently (with
each question) or give the learner the opportunity to suppress or request
the edit feature.

TYPES OF SCREENS

Screens can be described by their use in the lesson. Common screens
are the title screen, opening screen, direction screen, test screen, lesson
screen, and termination screen.

Only one idea should be displayed on a screen. You may therefore
need more than one screen for each use.

- If you are using any of these frequently, you can design a tem-
  plate, or master screen, for each so that you need not redesign the
  screen each time.

Title Screen

The title screen is the first screen displayed when the learner places the
diskette in the disc drive. The title screen may include a logo, the title
of the course, lesson, or module, and the author's name and affiliation,
publication date, and version or revision. The names and titles of the
instructional designer, programmer, graphic artist, or other design team
members should also be included (Fig. 5-6). Title screens should be in-
formative and attractively designed since they are the learner's first introduction to you and the instruction.

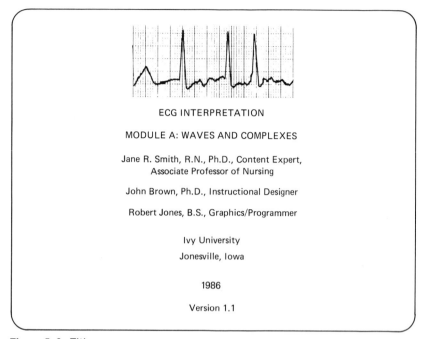

ECG INTERPRETATION

MODULE A: WAVES AND COMPLEXES

Jane R. Smith, R.N., Ph.D., Content Expert,
Associate Professor of Nursing

John Brown, Ph.D., Instructional Designer

Robert Jones, B.S., Graphics/Programmer

Ivy University

Jonesville, Iowa

1986

Version 1.1

Figure 5-6. Title screen.

Opening Screen

The opening or introductory screen is used to engage the learner in the
CAI lesson. Here is your opportunity to catch the learner's eye, arouse
curiosity, and increase motivation. Opening screens can serve as advance
organizers to establish the framework for instruction. You can also personalize instruction at this time by asking the learner to tell you his or
her name (Fig. 5–7).

Direction Screen

More information is needed before the lesson can begin. The direction
screens are used to give an overview of the lesson or establish the purpose, goals, and objectives of the lesson. They also give instructions on
how to proceed through the lesson and how to enter information and
obtain help if needed. Direction screens should be succinct because learners are usually ready to begin the lesson as soon as possible.

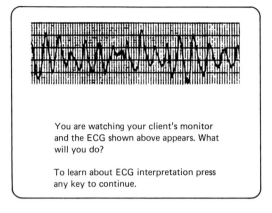

You are watching your client's monitor
and the ECG shown above appears. What
will you do?

To learn about ECG interpretation press
any key to continue.

Figure 5-7. Opening screen.

Test Screen

If you are using a pretest or entry test with your lesson, include the test screen before the lesson screen. Screens for posttests, of course, are placed after the lesson.

Lesson Screen

Lesson screens are used for the tutorial, drill and practice, simulation, or test. Examples of screen designs for these teaching strategies are given in Chapters 7 through 10.

- Use only one teaching strategy per lesson.

Lesson screens are further described as teaching screens or response screens. Teaching screens are used to present instruction. Response screens ask the learner to respond to a question and display feedback.

Termination Screen

The termination screen signals the end of the lesson. If the lesson was scored, this is an appropriate place to display the score. Termination screens can be used to give further instructions to the learner about obtaining remedial or supplementary information. Author names, series logo, and an invitation to the learner to study with you again can also be placed on this last screen.

SCREEN LAYOUT

It is not sufficient to write an excellent lesson; you must also arrange it carefully on the screen. Orienting information, directions, lessons and/or responses, error messages, and options must be available to the learner as needed and are placed in a designated place on the screen known as functional area or screen window (Heines, 1984; Larson, 1984). Each type of information appears in the same place on each screen (Fig. 5-8). All information does not need to be displayed at all times but should be available if the learner requests it.

Orienting Information

Orienting information is used to let the learner know what lesson is being used and, if the lesson is lengthy, to locate the learner's place in the lesson. Orienting information serves the same function as a table of contents, chapter headings, and page numbers in a book. Since the learner cannot scan titles or flip pages you will need to provide this information on the screen.

Orienting information is placed on the screen in an unobtrusive place (Fig. 5-9). If the lesson is long or if a score is displayed this information can be displayed as well.

Orienting information is helpful when revising the lesson or directing the learner to remedial help. It is much easier to find references to screen numbers than a general place in a lesson.

Directions

Directions inform the learner what to do and how to use the lesson. Here you will tell the learner how to use keys to enter information, how to respond, and how to continue. Directions should be clearly written and placed on the screen in a prominent place (Fig. 5-10).

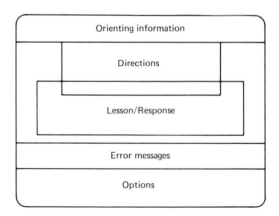

Figure 5-8. Screen layout.
Note six functional areas.

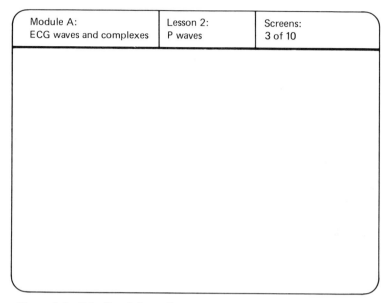

Module A: ECG waves and complexes	Lesson 2: P waves	Screens: 3 of 10

Figure 5-9. Orienting information.

Lesson Text

The lesson text is the central focus of the screen. Narrative and graphic displays are placed here. Lesson text should be arranged so that all related text is in one place. Paging or scrolling or "wrapping" around other screen areas is disruptive to reading.

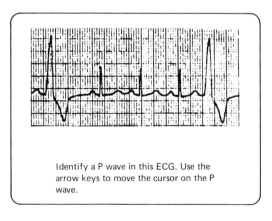

Identify a P wave in this ECG. Use the arrow keys to move the cursor on the P wave.

Figure 5-10. Screen directions.

Response/Feedback

An area of the screen is also used to receive the learner's response and give feedback. Since the lesson and response/feedback do not appear on the screen at the same time, the same central area used for the lesson text can also be used for learner response and feedback.

Error Messages

A functional area of the screen is reserved for error messages to learners who are having difficulty entering a response or following a lesson. Error messages such as "You entered a letter, please enter a number and try again" appear in the designated screen area (Fig. 5-8).

Some CAI authors use auditory devices such as a bell to signal error. This approach is discouraged for adult learners who are using the computer in the presence of classmates, co-workers, or the instructor.

Options

Options for screen display are used to give the learner control with the lesson. Typical options are to move the screen up or down, to ask for help, to exit (quit) the lesson, to see another screen, or to review the lesson or section. Since options are only necessary if the learner needs them, they should be placed at the bottom of the screen where they are visible but unobtrusive (Fig. 5-11).

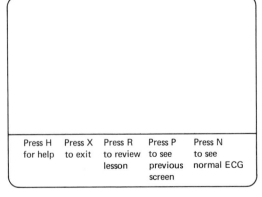

Figure 5-11. Screen options.

SPECIAL TECHNIQUES

There are several techniques that can be used to make the screen attractive, to cue or highlight significant information, or to display diagrams or show movement. Use of these techniques is dependent on the capabilities of the computer and the flexibility of the programming language or authoring system. A graphic artist is a helpful member of the design team as you create these special effects.

Inverse Video

Inverse (reverse) video is created by reversing the foreground and background colors (Fig. 5–12). The words enclosed in the inverse colors are highlighted for the learner and are useful for giving attention to a word or cuing.

- Leave an extra space before and after the last letter in the word so the preceding and following words do not run into the shaded portion of the video.
- Avoid overuse of this technique; effectiveness is destroyed by repetition.

Foreground/Background

Reversing the foreground and background is another technique to attract attention and cue the learner. This special effect is useful with diagrams and to show changes resulting from health care action.

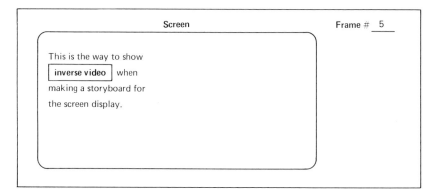

Figure 5–12. Storyboard showing inverse video.

Underline

The simple effect of underlining is easily obtained and is often a satis-factory way to draw attention to key words. Underlining is useful in tests to emphasize words such as *"not"* or *"never."*

Highlights

Another way to draw attention to key words or parts of a diagram is to highlight them with boxes, brackets or special style letters (fonts) (Fig. 5-13). This effect is useful in tutorials to emphasize significance or when giving feedback to shape, cue, or for reinforcement.

Blinking/Flashing

Movement of a letter or figure is a stunning device to catch the learner's attention. This technique can be used to cue or direct attention.

- Use blinking in only one area of the screen at a time.
- Use blinking sparingly because it can be distracting as well as at-tracting.

Graphics

Television, movies, and video games have geared learners to expect in-teresting visual displays on screens. Most design experts believe the screen designs for CAI should be equally interesting and recommend using a graphic design or otherwise creating a visually interesting screen using space and word arrangements for *each* screen display in a CAI lesson (Sweeters, 1985).

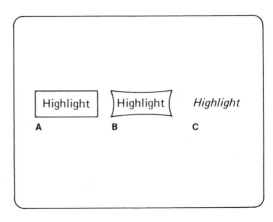

Figure 5-13. Highlights.
A. Box. **B.** Brackets.
C. Fonts.

Graphics have instructional value for motivating learners, showing relationships, and displaying results of action. Another powerful use of graphic designs is to provide an organizing framework to enhance memory (Fig. 5-14). Graphics should therefore be used to instruct, rather than entertain.

The use of graphics is limited by screen resolution, color, and availability of programming language or a graphics editor component of an authoring system. Graphics increase the cost of developing your lesson, so be certain that their use is justified.

- Textual descriptions should be placed under the diagram on the screen.
- When real-life visual representation is needed in your lesson, include these in a student workbook, or refer the student to slides, photographs, or videotape/disc.
- To decrease cost of graphic art, place graphics in a workbook.

Movement

Movement, or animation, can be used in your lesson to show action, changes, or to demonstrate some psychomotor skills. As with graphic

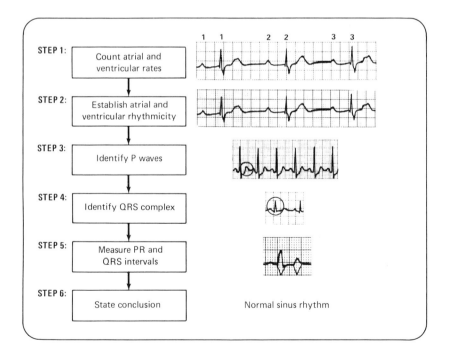

Figure 5-14. Graphics used to enhance memory.

art, movement is expensive to program owing to the time involved and the need for a significant amount of system memory. The detail of the motion, furthermore, depends on the screen resolution (greater detail with higher resolution) and the need for movement should be considered during the planning stages to assure appropriate hardware configuration and design team expertise.

- Lifelike and realistic motion is best shown with videotape or movies. Consider using these as adjuncts to the lesson to show movement, or create the lesson using interactive video technique.

Color

Color provides a contrast on the screen that attracts the eye and is therefore useful for highlighting, cuing, and showing criterial elements. Color is also useful in providing a change in stimuli and thereby decreases boredom and increases motivation. Too many color changes, however, can be distracting, and the CAI author should plan the use of color at the outset of the lesson design. Generally, colors should be limited to seven and used consistently throughout the lesson (Sweeters, 1985).

Color is also an expensive and time-consuming addition to the lesson and requires the use of a color monitor for lesson use. You should determine the need for color at the outset of the lesson design; tests and some simulations, for example, would not mandate the use of color.

When color is used, red and blue are the best surface colors for adults (Fleming & Levie, 1978). These colors do not always contrast well and these and all colors should be tested during development and again during developmental testing with the target audience.

Space

The space (blank space, "white space") on the screen can be used effectively to provide contrast and emphasis. Space and the arrangement of words can be used to show hierarchical arrangements or relationships (Fig. 5-15). The lines between paragraphs are another use of space to visually separate information or concepts. Margin space can also be used to highlight key words. Generally, however, the left margin should be justified (made even), while the right margin should be ragged.

Eye movement across the screen should also influence use of space and placement of information. The learner's eye movement is from the top left of the screen to the lower right of the screen. The most important information should therefore be placed in these locations (Fig. 5-16). Least important information should be placed in the lower left corner of the screen or otherwise highlighted since normal eye movement only scans that area.

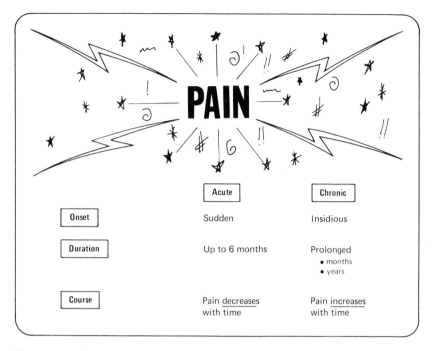

Figure 5-15. Use of space to establish order.

Overlay

Another screen design technique is the use of the overlay, or placement of parts of one screen over another. This technique can be used to decrease clutter and memory load when more than seven items must be displayed. Here the designer can create the diagram and include several words on one screen and then add other labels, text, or diagrams on the

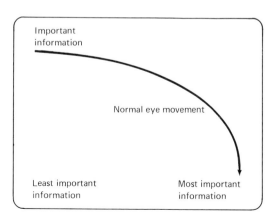

Figure 5-16. Placement of information on screen to maximize normal eye movement.

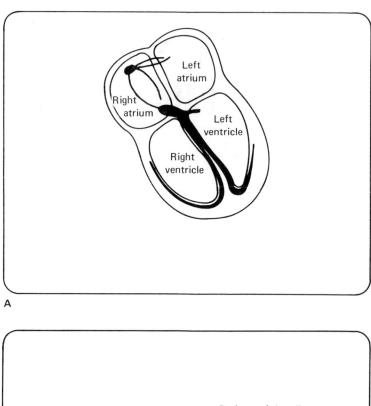

A

B

SA node

Bachmann's bundle

Internodal pathways

AV junction

Bundle of His

Purkinje fibers

In normal cardiac conduction impulses travel from the SA node to the left atrium via Bachmann's bundle and down the internodal pathways to the AV junction, the bundle of His, and to purkinje fibers.

Figure 5-17. Overlay screen. **A**. First screen. **B**. Overlay.

overlay screen (Fig. 5–17). Overlay screens should be designed to appear with emphasis to the learner, with different color or letter style so the change is apparent. Overlays or return to the previous screen should be in the learner's control so he or she can return to view previous screens.

WRITING STYLE

The writing style used in CAI lessons is different from that of textbooks. Learners attribute a personality to the computer (Jay, 1983) and you can help give it a good one by writing as if you were talking to the learner. Write in the second person, using "you" and refer to yourself as "I." You can also personalize the lesson by asking the learner's name at the beginning of the lesson and using it occasionally with directions or feedback.

Writing for CAI is lean. Use concrete language and keep the sentences short. The sentence should begin with the subject first and follow with the predicate. This decreases memory load for the learner and helps focus attention.

Jargon and slang is to be avoided in CAI writing. Medical terminology includes words that may not be familiar to all learners. If the lesson is being used by a client be certain no unfamiliar words are used.

Humor is a touchy subject in CAI writing. What is funny for you may not be to the learner. If you incorporate humor, test it with the target audience before leaving it in the lesson.

Feedback must be written in a form that avoids denigrating the learner. A positive tone should be used to give correction.

Several guidelines can be used for spacing text on the screen (Fig. 5–18). Upper- and lowercase letters are used as is natural. In most instances text is single-spaced with double-space between paragraphs or for a break in thought. Lines on the screen should be short (8 to 10 words per line) for adult learners (Heines, 1984). The text should not cover the entire screen and natural phrases should be kept together.

SUMMARY

The visual interpretation of your CAI lesson on the CRT screen is one of the most important aspects of lesson design. You should be cognizant of your computer's screen configuration and resolution as you begin to design the lesson. Screen commands facilitate communication between the CAI author, the computer, and the learner. Carefully constructed menus, prompts, error messages, and editing capabilities can help even the most novice computer user progress through a lesson. Screens are

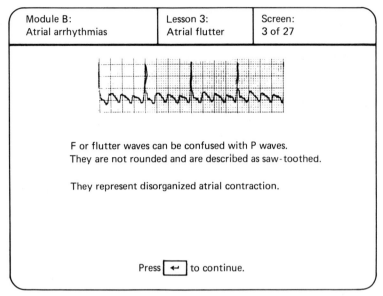

Module B: Atrial arrhythmias	Lesson 3: Atrial flutter	Screen: 3 of 27

F or flutter waves can be confused with P waves.
They are not rounded and are described as saw-toothed.

They represent disorganized atrial contraction.

Press [↵] to continue.

NOTE:
- Text under graphics
- 8 to 10 words/line
- Natural upper- and lowercase letters
- Single-space lines
- Double-space paragraphs

Figure 5-18. Text spacing on screen.

used to introduce the lesson, engage the learner's attention, inform the learner of the purpose, goals, objectives of the lesson, give a test, present the lesson, and indicate lesson termination. Information on the screen is displayed in a functional area. The orienting information directions, text, learner response/feedback, error messages, and options must be located in a consistent place where the learner can find them. Special techniques such as inverse video, foreground/background reverses, underlining, highlights, blinking, graphics, movement, color, space, and overlay are used to increase instructional effectiveness of the lesson. Since they are time consuming and expensive to create they should be used to meet instructional intents. Finally, the writing style used in CAI text is different from expository writing. Sentences are short and to the point and written as dialogue to the learner. Screens give life to your lesson, so animate them!

CHECKLIST: SCREEN DESIGN

Screen commands:

1. Menus
   a. Title, option list, entry prompt included   _____
   b. Menus used to orient learner to overview of course, lesson, module   _____
   c. Menus used to inform learner of place in course, lesson, module   _____
   d. Submenus flow logically from main menus   _____
2. Prompts
   a. Prompt used to inform learner how to enter responses   _____
   b. Prompt display controlled by learner   _____
   c. Prompts used when needed   _____
3. Error message
   a. Available as needed by learner   _____
   b. Displayed consistently   _____
   c. Written to inform, not denigrate   _____
4. Edit
   a. Edit capabilities exist   _____
   b. Edit prompts are consistent   _____

Screen layout:

1. Orienting information
   a. Always present   _____
   b. Unobtrusive   _____
2. Directions
   a. Clearly written   _____
   b. Appear as early as needed in lesson   _____
   c. Prominent on screen   _____
3. Text/Response/Feedback
   a. Single-spaced, double-spaced for paragraphs   _____
   b. Centrally located on screen   _____
   c. Blocked to avoid paging, scrolling, wrapping   _____
4. Error messages
   a. Available if needed   _____
   b. Consistent placement on screen   _____
5. Options
   a. Available   _____
   b. Appropriate to lesson   _____
   c. Unobtrusive on screen   _____

Special techniques:
1. Used for instructional purposes _____
2. Support versus detract _____
3. Necessary (other media better?) _____

Writing style:
1. Engages learner _____
2. Clear, lean _____
3. Concrete _____
4. Humor appropriate _____
5. Language and terms at learner's reading level _____

REFERENCES

Fleming, M., & Levie, W. H. (1978). *Instructional message design*. Englewood Cliffs, N.J.: Educational Technology Publications.

Heines, J. (1984). *Screen design strategies for computer assisted instruction*. Bedford, Mass.: Digital Press.

Jay, T. (1983). The cognitive approach to computer courseware design and evaluation. *Educational Technology*, *23*(1), 22-25.

Larson, D. (1984). Effective screen designs for nursing CAI. *Computers in Nursing*, *2*, 224-227.

Sweeters, W. G. (1985). Screen design guidelines. In Proceedings of the 26th International ADCIS Conference. Bellingham, Wash.: Western Washington University.

Additional Readings

Burke, R. (1982). *CAI Sourcebook*. Englewood Cliffs, N.J.: Prentice-Hall.

Crawford, C. (1982). Design techniques and ideals for computer games. *Byte, 7* (12), 96-108.

DiGiammarino, F., Johnson, D., & Lowd, B. (1982). *Microcomputer use and software design*. Springfield, Mo.: Milton Bradley Co.

Godfrey, D., & Sterling, S. (1982). *The elements of CAI*. Reston, Va.: Reston.

Hathaway, M. (1984). Variables of computer screen display and how they affect learning. *Educational Technology*, *24*(1), 7-11.

Hausmann, K. (1981). Tips on writing instructional software for microcomputers. In J. Thomas (Ed.), *Microcomputers in the schools*. Phoenix: Onyx Press.

Kehrberg, K. (1981). Microcomputer software development: New strategies for a new technology. In J. Thomas (Ed.), *Microcomputers in the schools*. Phoenix: Onyx Press.

Landa, R. (1984). *Creating courseware*. New York: Harper & Row.

Simpson, H. (1982). A human-factors style guide for program design. *Byte, 7* (4), 108–132.

Spannaus, T. (1985). Screen design for CAI. In proceedings of the 26th International ADCIS Conference. Bellingham, Wash.: Western Washington University.

6

Authoring Tools

After the lesson is developed, the flowcharts and storyboards prepared, and the screen displays designed, it is necessary to translate these to the computer. Authoring tools are the means by which the lessons are coded for the computer. These tools are usually used by a computer programmer, but recently have been simplified for use by CAI authors. Regardless of the type of authoring tool you or the design team uses, you should be familiar with the advantages and disadvantages of the tools currently available and be prepared to make decisions about their use during the product formulation stage of lesson development.

AUTHORING TOOLS

There are several authoring tools that can be used singly or in combination to facilitate efficient and cost-effective lesson development. The most common are programming languages, authoring languages, authoring systems, and the various text and graphic editors and record-keeping systems that are used as adjuncts (Table 6-1). Another tool, primarily for use by instructional designers, is the instructional design system that is used to guide the development of pedagogically sound instruction. Most of these authoring tools are available for microcomputers and several are developed specifically for the diagnostic processes

TABLE 6-1. AUTHORING TOOLS

	Programming Language	Authoring Language	Authoring System
Time to learn	6–30 months	2–6 weeks	1–3 days
Time to develop lesson	200 hours	16 hours	16 hours
Personnel needed	Programmer	Programmer or CAI author	CAI author
Instructional strategies that can be used	All	Most	Limited
Revision of lesson	Difficult; requires programming	Difficult; requires programming	Easy; done with authoring system
Graphics	Available	Available	Not available with most systems

Adapted from CAI Development Aids; Elkridge, Mo.: Micronome, 1981, with permission.

used by physicians, nurses, and allied health care professionals (Grobe, 1984).

Programming Language

Programming language (general purpose programming language) is a specific language such as BASIC or PASCAL that is used to code the lesson to the computer. Each line of the lesson is written in a code that gives instructions to the computer about which tasks to perform, such as displaying information on the screen or performing calculations. Programming languages permit a wide range of flexibility for lesson design but require many commands to code each lesson. The major advantage of using a programming language is the ability to develop lessons with complex branching and unique graphic arts. The use of the programming language requires programming language skills and the time to code the lesson. In most instances it is advisable to use a computer programmer to code the lessons that require the use of the programming language.

Authoring Language

Authoring languages are simplified programming languages. They employ frequently used commands that are typically used to create lessons and judge learner responses. One authoring language used by educators is PILOT (Programmed Instruction Learning or Teaching) or DAL (Digital Authoring Language). Some flexibility is lost with authoring languages as compared to programming language, but development costs are less because of the decreased time involved in producing a lesson. Authoring languages take from 2 to 6 weeks to learn and require knowledge of coding and programming procedures. Authoring languages are usually used by a programmer, rather than the author. The software for programming languages is readily available.

Authoring Systems

Authoring systems, or author-prompting systems, are computer programs or systems software that have been designed to create other programs. They have a standard format that corresponds to a typical lesson. The author is guided through the system by supplying information as the questions (prompts) appear on the screen. Typical prompts are for text display, questions, responses to accept, and feedback to give.

There are several types of authoring systems, described as prompt driven, menu driven, or program driven. *Prompt-driven* systems provide on-screen questions and the author supplies the answers (Table 6–2). A standard sequence is followed in prompt-driven authoring systems, thus limiting creativity. *Menu-driven* systems, on the other hand, provide options for lesson format at several levels. The first menu gives choices about lessons and subsequent menus give additional choices about lesson sequence. The lesson can be varied with text and graphics. *Programming systems* use authoring languages that extend the flexibility for lesson design. These systems are more difficult to learn but increase the speed by which lessons can be developed.

There are advantages and disadvantages of using authoring systems. The main advantages are the savings in time and production costs. Authoring systems also permit CAI authors to develop their own lessons without the support of a programmer. Another advantage is the ease with which lessons can be revised because extensive programming is not required.

The primary disadvantage is the loss of flexibility in instructional design and the limited use of a variety of instructional strategies. Most authoring systems are developed for a drill and practice format which guides the author to enter text, enter questions, enter responses, and enter feedback for responses; rules are usually followed by examples. In these formats the branching and remediation are limited.

Currently, several authoring systems are available for authoring courseware specific to the instructional needs of health care professionals. Before purchasing an authoring system you should be aware of your own CAI courseware requirements and the features of a given system.

Authoring systems have various features. When evaluating these systems it is important to note and compare the type of instructional strat-

TABLE 6-2. PROMPT-DRIVEN AUTHORING SYSTEM

PROMPT	
AUTHOR INPUT	**Name of Lesson:** Teaching clients about digitalis drugs
	Text to be Displayed: After using this lesson you will be able to instruct clients about side effects of digitalis drugs.
	Question 1: Which of the following should you teach an adult client about the effect of digitalis on heart rate? 1. "You may gain weight, so report a gain of 2 pounds to your physician." 2. "Your heart beat may slow down, so take your pulse every day and tell your physician if it is less than 60 beats per minute." 3. "Your heart rate may increase, so take your pill with orange juice."
	Feedback for Correct Response: 2. Correct. Digitalis can cause slowing of A-V conduction. Press space bar to continue.
	Feedback for Incorrect Responses: 1. Incorrect. Digitalis has a diuretic effect and the client should *lose* weight. Neither minimal weight gain nor loss should greatly affect heart rate. Try another response. 3. Incorrect. You must be thinking about preventing the side effects of hypokalemia. Try another response.

egy, the learner management capabilities, instructional features, technical features and system requirements, user-support, and cost. A checklist is included at the end of this chapter for your use in evaluating authoring systems.

The instructional strategy in most authoring systems is limited to one or two, usually drill and practice or tutorial. If you are designing instruction for simulations, or a wide variety of instructional strategies, be certain the authoring system has the flexibility you need.

Most authoring systems permit you to include learner management capabilities such as record keeping and scoring. Again, you should be familiar with your needs and compare them with those offered by the authoring system.

The main disadvantage of authoring systems is the limited use of instructional features, such as sequence, feedback, opportunity for interaction and practice, opportunity for learner control, and the ability to create motivating instruction and screen design. Examine the system you are considering for the presence of these features and weigh the tradeoffs you might make in terms of saving programming time compared with loss of pedagogical effectiveness.

The technical features and system requirements of an authoring system must be matched with the computer you currently have or are considering purchasing as well as the type of CAI courseware you are developing. Factors to consider are the configuration of the computer, the need for peripheral devices, the use of text and graphics editors, and the networking with other computers.

Most vendors of authoring systems provide user-support with the system. The support may include training, tutorials, documentation, and even instructional design support. Be certain that you have an on-site demonstration and trial before you purchase the system. Discussing the system with other users is also advised to obtain firsthand information about the usability of the system and vendor support.

The costs of authoring systems vary considerably and of course depend on what is included in the package price. One issue of interest to CAI authors is the license agreement and the ownership of the copyright of any courseware developed using the authoring system. Currently, several publishers of authoring systems retain rights to sales of courseware with compensation given to the author. If you are considering marketing your courseware it is important to understand the license fee requirements.

Text Editors

Text editors are systems software that provides the CAI author or programmer with the mechanism for building text files for screen displays and lessons such as drill and practice items. The text editors permit editing of text as it appears on the computer screen. This tool is useful because it permits authors to revise screen designs as they develop the lesson because it is possible to see the placement of text on the screen as it is developed. Some text editors have choices for size of type, upper- and lowercase letters, and color. If you are considering using a text editor be certain it will support the type of lessons you will be creating.

Graphics Editors

Graphics editors are systems software used to create visual displays on the screen. They have preplotted designs so that one key press will produce a figure such as a line, circle, or box. Graphics editors also provide colors and may be able to fill in or shade designs with color. Graphics editors vary as to color options, resolution, and graphics but may be limited in their capacity for creating figures or diagrams needed in health professional education. The main advantage of the graphics editor, as with the text editor, is that you can see on-screen what will be in the lesson and graphic displays and color can be adjusted during the design stage of lesson development.

Record-keeping Systems

Some authoring tools have record-keeping systems and student management systems for computer managed instruction. These systems, incorporated with the lesson, are used to direct the student through a training program or to administer a pre- or posttest or a final examination. They can accept a student's name or identification number, track student-use time as well as the student's progress through a lesson or course. These records are useful for evaluating student progress and CAI lesson use.

Instructional Design Systems

Instructional design systems are more sophisticated than authoring systems; they are, in fact, able to guide the instructional design of the lesson (Merrill & Wood, 1984). These systems are being developed to be used by instructional designers so that lesson design can be simplified and standardized. The main advantage of these systems is the ability to incorporate learning principles in lesson design and assure courseware based on learning theory.

ADVANTAGES AND DISADVANTAGES OF USING AUTHORING TOOLS

Authoring tools are currently being developed and revised as CAI is used as a significant medium of instruction. There are advantages as well as disadvantages of these tools and the user must be able to justify purchase (see Table 6–1).

Advantages

The main advantage of using an authoring tool is to save time. Lessons which previously took 100 to 200 hours to create can now be developed in 10 to 20 hours. Time can be freed therefore for careful lesson design and evaluation.

Another advantage of using authoring tools is the use of personnel. Courseware authors can easily become lesson programmers, thus saving hiring a computer programmer and increasing productivity and individualizing lessons for specific learner groups.

Disadvantages

Authoring tools are not panaceas for CAI lesson development and they do not eliminate the need for lesson design, development, and evaluation. A major criticism of authoring tools, particularly authoring systems, is the lack of flexibility. Lesson designs become routine, and branching, adaptive testing, and creative graphics are lost for the sake of rapid and easy lesson production.

Another significant disadvantage of authoring systems is the absence of learning theory and the use of an instructional design science. Because most tools are restricted to one instructional framework, teaching–learning theories appropriate to the learner may not be included.

SUMMARY

Authoring tools are used to transform lesson plans into computer programs. There are six main tools: programming language, authoring language, authoring systems, text editors, graphics editors, and instructional design systems. Each tool has advantages and disadvantages. CAI authors are well advised to determine their needs for authoring tools and to select those that meet specific lesson design needs prior to lesson development. A checklist is included at the end of this chapter to guide your evaluation of authoring systems.

CHECKLIST: EVALUATING AUTHORING SYSTEMS

Instructional strategy:
1. Drill and practice   _____
2. Tutorial   _____
3. Simulation   _____
4. Testing   _____

Learner management capabilities:
1. Learner management   _____
2. Record keeping
   a. Learner names   _____
   b. Time spent   _____

3. Scoring
   a. Total score   _____
   b. Component Scores   _____
   c. Item analysis   _____

Instructional features:

1. Sequence
   a. Compatible with instructional specifications   _____
   b. Exit, enter capabilities   _____
   c. Branching capabilities   _____
2. Feedback
   a. Immediate, delayed   _____
   b. For correct and incorrect response   _____
   c. Can be varied   _____
3. Interaction and practice
   a. Unit size can be varied   _____
   b. Practice opportunities frequent and variable   _____
   c. Misspelling allowance   _____
4. Learner control
   a. Pace, sequence   _____
   b. Exit, enter options   _____
5. Motivation
   a. Can individualize with learner name   _____
   b. Graphics support instruction   _____

Technical features/system requirements:

1. Type of computer used   _____
2. Configuration of computer needed
   a. Disk drives   _____
   b. Memory   _____
   c. Screen resolution   _____
   d. Input devices (keyboard, joystick, touch screen,
      mouse)   _____
3. Peripheral devices
   a. Graphics tablet   _____
   b. Audio   _____
   c. Videodisk/videotape   _____
   d. Printer   _____
4. Text editor
   a. Text Size   _____
   b. Upper-, lowercase text   _____
   c. Boldface, underline   _____
   d. Background/foreground   _____
   e. Spellchecker   _____

 5. Graphics editor
    a. Color   ____
    b. Resolution   ____
    c. Blinking, inverse video   ____
    d. Templates   ____
 6. Networking with other computers   ____

User-support:

 1. Training program available
    a. Time needed   ____
    b. Follow-up support; access to publisher   ____
 2. Instructional design support available   ____
 3. Tutorial provided   ____
 4. Documentation available
    a. User, technical   ____
    b. Complete, comprehensible   ____
 5. On-site trial before purchase   ____
 6. References to previous/current users   ____

Cost:

 1. Purchase/rental price
    a. Includes back-up disk, documentation   ____
    b. Includes training, ongoing support   ____
 2. Maintenance, repairs   ____
 3. License fee
    a. Institutional   ____
    b. User   ____
    c. Can market courseware developed with authoring system?   ____

REFERENCES

Grobe, S. (1984). Computer assisted instruction, an alternative. *Computers in Nursing*, *2*, 92–97.

Merrill, D., & Wood, L. (1984). Computer guided instructional design. *Journal of Computer-Based Instruction*, *11*, 60–63.

Additional Readings

Gayestic, D., & Williams, P. (1982). How "authoring" programs help you create interactive CAI. *Training*, *19*(8), 32–35.

Gerhold, G. (1980). Teacher-produced CAI. In R. Lewis, & E. Tagg (Eds.), *Computer Assisted Learning*. New York: North-Holland Publishing Co.

Kleiman, G., & Humphrey, M. (1982). Writing your own software, authoring tools make it easy. *Electronic Learning, 1*(5), 37–41.

Locatis, C., & Carr, V. (1985). Selecting authoring systems. *Journal of Computer-Based Instruction, 12*, 28–33.

Mudrick, D., & Stone, D. (1984). An adaptive authoring system for computer based instruction. *Journal of Computer-Based Instruction, 11*, 82–84.

Scandura, J. (1981). Microcomputer systems for authoring, diagnosis and instruction in rule based subject matter. *Educational Technology, 21*(1), 13–19.

Wasserman, A., & Girtz, G. (1982). The future of programming. *Communications of the ACM, 25*, 196–206.

Young, J. (1984). The case for using authoring systems to develop courseware. *Educational Technology, 24*(10), 26–31.

7

Designing Drill and Practice Exercises

Many teaching–learning activities in the health care professions require repeated practice to attain knowledge or skill proficiency. Drill and practice exercises are one teaching strategy to assist learners in achieving desired competence. After reading this chapter you will be able to recognize the design concept for drill and practice exercises and identify instructional uses for this CAI strategy. You will also be able to use the instructional design model to formulate the product, write the instructional specifications, design the lesson, and try, revise, and use your drill and practice lesson with your own learners.

DRILL AND PRACTICE EXERCISES

Drill and practice exercises are random or semirandom presentations of questions that require a response from the learner. Feedback is used to inform the learner of the correctness of the response. These exercises are used as repetition to reinforce facts and concepts after the content has been presented, usually in a textbook or lecture.

Design Concept

The design concept of drill and practice exercises involves questions, learner responses, and feedback about the response. Although some drill and practice exercises use the same questions and feedback until the student attains mastery, it is more effective to maximize the capability of the computer and incorporate teaching–learning principles in the lesson, by separating the questions into three pools: an item pool, a working pool, and a review pool (Salisbury, 1984) (Fig. 7–1).

The *item pool* consists of the entire list of questions. These questions are presented a few at a time as the student practices with the items.

The items the student is currently learning are cycled into the *working pool*. If the list is long it is advisable to limit this pool and add from the item pool as the working pool is mastered. Items in the working pool are presented randomly unless learning objectives are written for discrimination, in which case the items to be discriminated should be presented sequentially.

Items the learner has answered correctly are placed in a *review pool*. The learner therefore need not work with items already learned. To reinforce learning for the review items, however, these questions can be asked quickly at the beginning of the lesson and, if necessary, missed questions can be returned to the working pool.

Instructional Uses

Since many facts and skills must be learned to automaticity, drill and practice exercises are ideal for repetitious tasks. They can be used to review basic anatomy, calculate drug dose or I V drip rates, review terminology, practice ECG interpretation, or learn side effects of drugs. Drill and practice exercises can be used for instructing clients about diet lists or side effects of drugs.

Drill and practice exercises on the computer have several advantages for adult learners. Practice can be done with privacy at the learner's own pace. Learning time may also be decreased when efficient drill practices as described above are used.

PRODUCT FORMULATION

As with any instructional product development, lesson design begins with product formulation. Time, money, and resources should be identified before developing the drill and practice exercise. An overview of the lesson in outline form is also prepared at this time.

Time, Money, and Resources

Drill and practice exercises are one of the more easily developed CAI strategies. Less time is needed for developing these lessons than for tutorials or simulations. Existing tests, matching exercises, or definitions can be used as the basis for the lesson, thus saving development time.

Outline

The outline for drill and practice exercises should include the questions, the correct response, and the feedback. The outline delimits the scope of the content and provides an estimate of lesson size.

INSTRUCTIONAL SPECIFICATIONS

Before creating the item pool for your drill and practice exercise you must identify the instructional specifications for your lesson. These include needs analysis, learner analysis, task analysis, purpose, goals and objectives, as well as the teaching–learning principles used in CAI drill and practice.

Needs Analysis

Drill and practice exercises are developed for expressed learning needs. Needs for drill and practice exercises generally evolve from performance discrepancies that can be solved by repeated practice.

Learner Analysis

To design drill and practice exercises you must know what previous knowledge the learner has acquired. This information can be obtained from a pretest or from evaluation of course materials and previous instruction.

rt

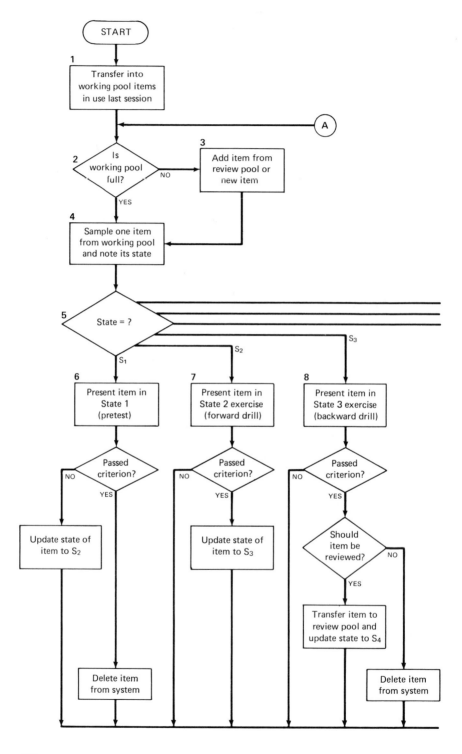

Task Analysis

Because the goal of drill and practice exercises is to increase automatic responses to task subskills it is necessary to conduct a task analysis to identify those subskills. In order to analyze ECGs, for example, the learner must first be able to recognize waves and complexes and discriminate between them. The subskills of recognizing P wave, T wave and QRS complex are, therefore, the subskills to be practiced before learning to interpret ECGs. Examples from a sufficient range of the subskills should be included in the item pool. It is also useful to identify the context in which subskills are used, in this case interpreting a client's ECG

Figure 7-1. Design concept: drill and practice. (From Salisbury, D. Strategies for designing drill and practice programs for computers. In proceedings of the 25th International ADCIS Conference. Bellingham, Wash.: Western Washington University, 1984, with permission.)

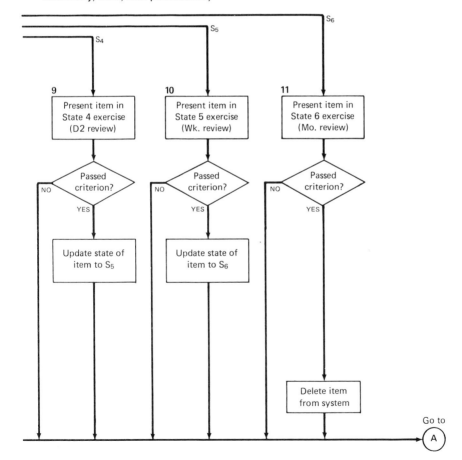

so the developer (and learner) can understand why the subskills must be mastered.

Purpose, Goals, and Objectives

The purpose of drill and practice exercises is to provide the learner with an opportunity to learn facts and concepts to a mastery or automatic level. Lesson goals are designed for the learner to attain lesson mastery. Objectives in drill and practice are usually written for lower cognitive levels of behavior and typically include objectives such as define, recognize, use, identify. Performance standards for objectives are written for 100 percent mastery.

Teaching–Learning Principles

Sequence, feedback, learner control, and motivation are the primary pedagogical considerations of drill and practice exercises. Deliberate decisions must be made to include these in each drill and practice lesson.

Sequence. Elements of instruction in drill and practice exercises are sequenced to ask questions, obtain learner response, give feedback and remediate (try again later), or progress to the next question until all questions are mastered.

The sequence of presenting questions in drill and practice exercises depends on the design of instruction. In simple lessons a random order may be used. If the list of questions is long and complex, however, it may be preferable to divide the questions into an item pool, working pool, and review pool. The sequence of questions then depends on the learner's ability to master the items. Sequencing may also be accomplished by identifying the item difficulty during task analysis (see Chap. 3) and then ordering the items from easy to difficult.

Feedback. Each response in a drill and practice exercise is given feedback. Correct responses are acknowledged with a statement indicating the learner has made the correct response.

Incorrect responses can be acknowledged in several ways. One is to inform the learner the response was incorrect and direct the learner to try again. This approach assumes the learner can correct the response and attempt to give a correct response, but it also encourages guessing. Another way to acknowledge incorrect responses is to provide information about why the response was incorrect. This both teaches and corrects mistakes. Feedback here can focus on the knowledge and the process the student used to obtain the response. The student is ultimately directed to try a parallel question to assure that the student has mastered the item.

Learner Control. Learner control can be incorporated in drill and practice exercises by giving the learner options about categories of questions to answer, mastery levels to set, and when to quit. Since drill and practice exercises can be potentially endless, provide the learner with an exit option.

Motivation. Drill and practice exercises are boring for some students. Questions and answers should be short and relevant. Competition such as establishing scoring levels or making a game for the drill can increase the challenge of this lesson. The value of rote learning can be demonstrated to the learner by following the drill with a tutorial or simulation based on the facts learned during the drill.

SCREEN DESIGN

Screen format should be consistent for each question and for the feedback. Using numbers or Y/N simplifies input. If short answers are used they should appear at a consistent point on the screen. Screen design can contribute to maintaining motivation. Use of space and graphic design can add interest to an otherwise dull lesson.

LESSON DESIGN

The steps of lesson design for a drill and practice exercise are to write the directions, develop questions, establish responses, and design feedback. If a game, scoring, or other record-keeping procedures are to be used they should be designed at this time.

1. Directions. Directions are given to the learner during one of the first screens in the lesson. Directions inform the learner of the purpose, goals, and objectives of the lesson. They also indicate to the learner how to make and enter the response (Fig. 7-2). It may be necessary to inform the learner of how to correct an entry error.

2. Questions and Responses. The questions should be written clearly. The expected response should be discernible but involve more cognitive activity than "yes" or "no." Open-ended questions encourage more active thinking but are difficult to construct, particularly when the range

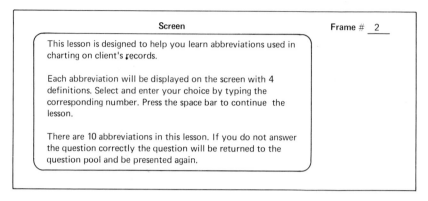

Figure 7-2. Directions for a drill and practice exercise.

of acceptable answers is wide. Multiple response questions with thoughtful distractors are an acceptable compromise (Fig. 7–3).

3. Feedback. Feedback is designed for each question (Fig. 7–4). The extent of feedback depends on the nature of the content and the maturity of the learner and can range from simply informing the learner the response was correct/incorrect to discussions of reasons for the incorrect response.

4. Scoring. A scoring system should be inherent in any drill and practice exercise (Fig. 7–5). The score can be presented as the number correct/ number incorrect. The score can be given for modules, for subsections of a lesson, or for a category of responses, such as terminology. The score can be kept on an ongoing basis and displayed continuously or on request of the learner. It is also appropriate to display the score at the end of the lesson. If the score is used for diagnostic and prescriptive purposes you may develop a tracking and record-keeping system as well.

TRYOUT, REVISION, AND USE

The tryout, revision, and use cycle described in Chapter 3 is used to assure lesson accuracy and desirable learner response.

When the lesson is used you can keep a record of how much time is spent with the lesson and how the learner responds. Use of drill and practice lessons can also be correlated with application lessons such as simulations.

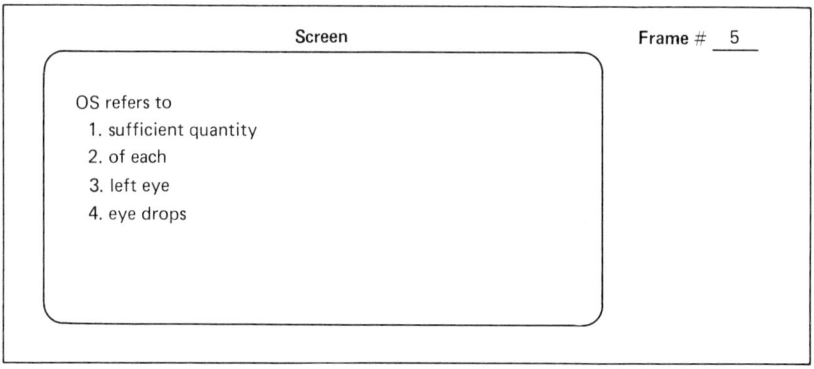

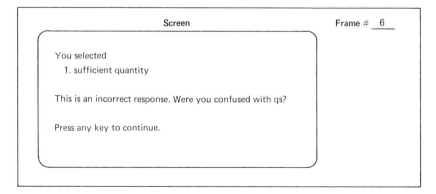

Screen   Frame # __5__

OS refers to
1. sufficient quantity
2. of each
3. left eye
4. eye drops

A

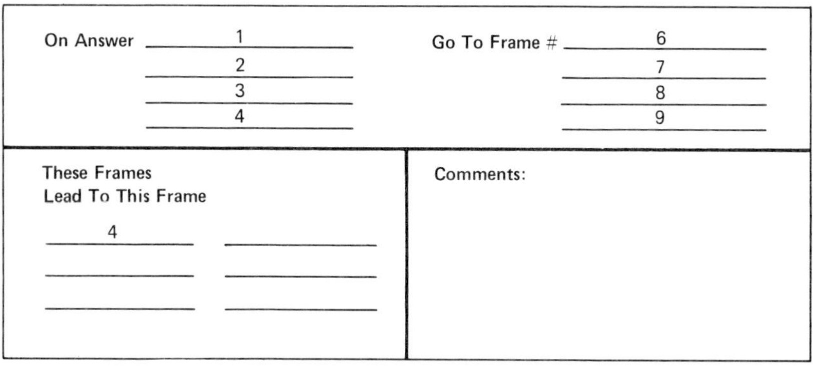

On Answer __1__   Go To Frame # __6__
__2__   __7__
__3__   __8__
__4__   __9__

These Frames
Lead To This Frame
__4__ _____

Comments:

B

Figure 7–3. Questions for drill and practice exercises (**A** and **B**).

Screen   Frame # __6__

You selected
1. sufficient quantity

This is an incorrect response. Were you confused with qs?

Press any key to continue.

Figure 7–4. Feedback drill and practice exercises.

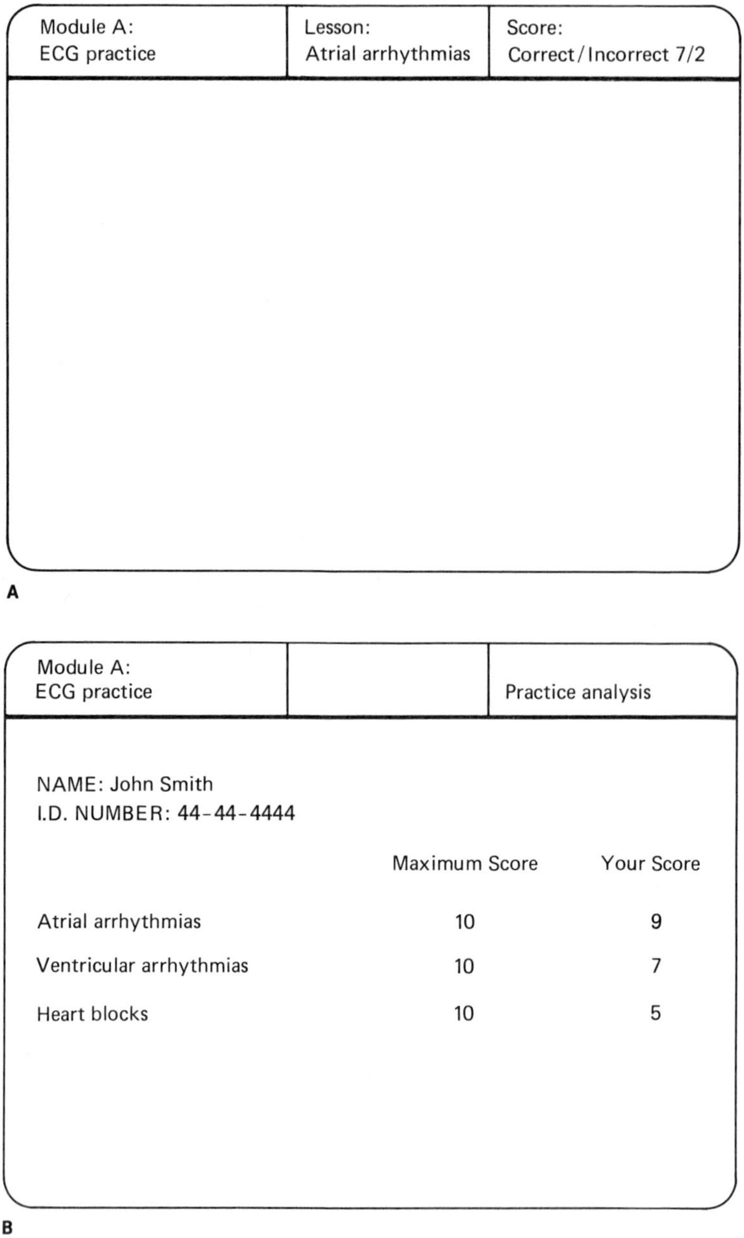

126

Module A: ECG practice	Lesson: Atrial arrhythmias	Score: Correct/Incorrect 7/2

A

Module A: ECG practice		Practice analysis

NAME: John Smith
I.D. NUMBER: 44-44-4444

	Maximum Score	Your Score
Atrial arrhythmias	10	9
Ventricular arrhythmias	10	7
Heart blocks	10	5

B

Figure 7-5. Scoring can be shown: **A.** continuously, **B.** at the end of the lesson.

SUMMARY

CAI drill and practice exercises give the learner an opportunity to master basic facts, concepts, and procedures. A design concept that maximizes the computer as a medium of instruction is one that separates items to be learned into three pools: the item pool, the working pool, and the review pool. Drill and practice are designed with attention given to product formulation, to writing instructional specifications, to designing an attractive screen, and clear lesson components. In the final design steps the author revises and uses the lesson to ensure the lesson assists learners in mastering facts and skills to a level of automatic performance. A checklist is included at the end of this chapter to guide the design of your drill and practice lesson.

CHECKLIST: DESIGNING DRILL
AND PRACTICE EXERCISES

Product formulation:
1. Development time allocated (50 to 100 hours)   _____
2. Outline prepared   _____

Instructional specifications:
1. Needs analysis   _____
2. Learner analysis
   a. Previous knowledge   _____
   b. Pretest   _____
3. Task analysis
   a. Subskills identified   _____
   b. Context for use of subskills established   _____
   c. Range of items adequate to represent all skills and subskills   _____
4. Purpose, goals, objectives
   a. Objectives written for lower levels of cognitive and psychomotor skills domains   _____
   b. Performance standards set at 100%   _____
5. Teaching–Learning principles used
   a. Logical sequence of questions (simple to complex)   _____
   b. Questions separated into item, working, review pools   _____
   c. All questions given feedback   _____

    d. Learner can control amount and pace of learning   _____
    e. Lesson is motivating   _____
    f. Content accurate   _____

Screen design:

    1. Consistent format for questions   _____
    2. Input options simplified   _____

Lesson design:

    1. Directions inform learner how to enter response   _____
    2. Questions and responses understood   _____
    3. Feedback for each question   _____
    4. Scoring system developed   _____

Tryout, revision, and use:

    1. Tryout
       a. Learner   _____
       b. Subject matter expert   _____
    2. Drill and practice revised before being used   _____
    3. Instructor and student manuals written   _____
    4. Program documentation written   _____
    5. Lesson used to consolidate learning of facts, concepts   _____

REFERENCE

Salisbury, D. (1984). Strategies for designing drill and practice programs for computers. In Proceedings of the 25th International ADCIS Conference. Bellingham, Wash.: Western Washington University.

Additional Readings

Friend, J., & Milojovic, J. (1984). Designing interactions between students and computers. In D. Walker & R. Hess (Eds.), *Instructional software: Principles and perspectives for design and use.* Belmont, Calif.: Wadsworth.

Godfrey, D., & Sterling, S. (1982). *The elements of CAI.* Reston, Va.: Reston.

Landa, R. (1984). *Creating courseware.* New York: Harper & Row.

8

Designing Tutorials

CAI tutorials enable you to teach learners as individuals. Tutorials provide consistent, replicable instruction. Well-designed tutorials can even teach problem solving and challenge learners to identify and use their own learning strategies. After reading this chapter you will be able to identify linear and branching tutorial designs, allocate time, money, and resources for tutorial development, prepare an outline of a tutorial, write instructional specifications, design the entire lesson, and try, revise, and use your own instructional product.

TUTORIALS

Tutorials are the epitome of Socratic dialogue. They are your own conversation with each learner. You can teach content as well as demonstrate problem-solving strategies. Each tutorial lesson can be used by an infinite number of students who benefit from your individually sequenced and personalized instruction.

Design Concept

CAI tutorials include teaching statements, facts, and as many examples as are needed to make the statement clear to the learner. Teaching questions (as opposed to testing questions) are asked to validate the learner's understanding of the instruction or to lead the learner to discovery, insight, or hypothesis formation. Depending on the learner's response to the question he or she is either moved forward to the next teaching statement or returned to relearn the material or seek remedial assistance (Fig. 8-1). Tutorials are highly adaptive because the learner can progress through the instruction without delay if he or she comprehends the instruction or can be routed back for review or remediation.

Tutorials can be designed to be linear or branched (Fig. 8-1). In *linear* designs all learners are returned to the same instruction until the content is mastered. Linear designs can be used when the range of examples is small or there is a reason that all students should follow the

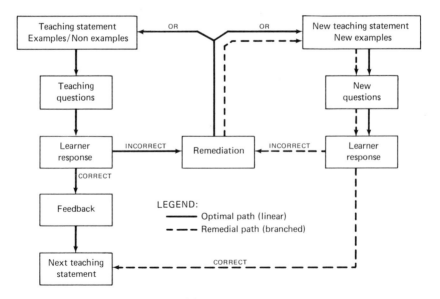

Figure 8-1. Design concept: tutorial.

same path, as in a procedure. In *branching* designs remediation is different from instruction. New statements and examples are used. It is in fact possible to create several branches for each statement so the learner has several options for learning. Branching also facilitates insight into mistakes as new examples are used and decreases boredom with instruction as well.

Instructional Use

Tutorials are used to teach facts, concepts, principles, or procedures. Tutorials can stand alone as the only method of instruction; they serve as a substitute for an assigned reading or a lecture.

Tutorials can also be used with other CAI. They can, for example, be used to present basic content, be followed by drill and practice exercises to establish automaticity, and when mastery is assured can be followed by simulations which provide the learner an opportunity to apply the material initially taught in the tutorial.

Tutorials are self-paced and the learner can spend as much time as necessary learning the lesson. For high achievers learning time is shortened while slower learners can progress without feeling rushed. Adult learners find tutorials an ideal way to learn because they are not threatened by failure and embarrassment. A tutorial is an ideal teaching strategy when the abilities of the learner group are varied.

PRODUCT FORMULATION

Developing effective tutorials requires planning. During the planning stage you will identify the time, money, and resources and make an outline of the tutorial lesson.

Time, Money, and Resources

Developing tutorials is time consuming. Although the time needed to design tutorials is less than for simulations (Schmidt & Lease, 1984), estimate 100 to 150 hours of development time for 1 hour of a tutorial. If your tutorial is complex you may wish to form a design team with other subject matter experts, an instructional designer, and a computer programmer.

Outline

The outline for a tutorial includes the instructional statements with examples and non examples, the teaching questions, and remediation with additional practice examples. Outlining at the outset facilitates lesson design in subsequent stages.

INSTRUCTIONAL SPECIFICATIONS

As with any instructional design, it is necessary to clearly identify the instructional specifications. These include needs analysis, learner analysis, task analysis, purpose, goals and objectives, and teaching–learning principles.

Needs Analysis

Tutorials are developed because there is a need in the curriculum or course for this type of instruction. The need may be related to deficits in instruction, variability of learners, or lack of faculty time for individualized instruction in certain content areas.

Learner Analysis

In order to be able to individualize the tutorial it is of utmost importance to have an understanding of the learner population. It will be necessary to know the learner's current knowledge base and skill level. It is also helpful to have insight into typical learner mistakes, misunderstandings, or areas of confusion when creating the remedial sections of the tutorial.

Task Analysis

The instructional task must be clearly identified in a tutorial. A task analysis (or skill or concept analysis) provides this information. Each component of the task analysis provides direction for instructional statements in the tutorial.

Purpose, Goals, and Objectives

The purpose of the tutorial is to assist the learner to acquire knowledge and skill or to develop an attitude. The goal is for the learner to learn the content. Objectives can be written at any level and at any performance standard.

Teaching–Learning Principles

There are four pedagogical principles used in designing tutorials. These are the use of sequence, interactivity and practice, feedback, and learner control.

Sequence. Sequence involves instructional statements to present content, followed by an example that clarifies, amplifies, or illuminates the instructional statement.

The next step of the tutorial is the teaching question, followed by learner response. Feedback is provided after each response and if the response is correct the learner progresses to the next section of the lesson; if incorrect the learner returns for remediation.

When teaching with examples it may also be useful to use non examples, or those items that are not examples of the instructional statement. T waves, which are not P waves but are often confused with them (by beginning students), for example, can be presented as non examples to further explicate the concept of P waves.

Interaction and Practice. Interaction with instructional materials serves to facilitate knowledge, attitude, or skill acquisition. Teaching questions that follow the instructional statement encourage this interaction. Here your creativity and tutorial skill is paramount. If the learner does not answer the question correctly it is possible to route the learner to more detailed instruction with additional examples and new questions for practice. The interaction should be appropriate to the task and may also involve solving a problem, selecting an action, or calculating a drug dose. Practice should be in the form in which the knowledge, skill, or attitude will be later tested.

Feedback. Feedback in tutorials is given after the teaching question. The learner should be informed that the response was correct or incorrect. When the response is incorrect you may also explain why the response was incorrect and coach, guide, or shape the learner to discover the mistake and how to correct it.

Learner Control. Learner control is a significant component of a tutorial. Learners should be able to determine which component of the tutorial they wish to study. Another way of using learner control is to permit learners to determine how many examples they need to learn the content. Some learners are able to grasp the content with one example and then move on; they become frustrated and bored viewing additional examples that may be useful to another student. Exit options should also be available.

Some learners are likely to leave the lesson before they have attained mastery (Tennyson & Buttry, 1980). They will continue, however, if they have meaningful information about progress toward objectives. Giving the learner information about progress (known as *advisement*) is easily incorporated in the tutorial and should be used when the goal of instruction is mastery or lesson completion.

SCREEN DESIGN

When designing the computer program for the tutorial, it is important that the screen does not look like a textbook. Information should be presented attractively on the screen. Graphic designs may be used to give examples and eliminate screen boredom.

Since tutorials are a dialogue between you and the student, design the lesson to accept student responses without frustration. Multiple choice responses to teaching questions are easier to use, when answers may have a wide range of acceptability. Open-ended or short-answer questions may also be used effectively. Error messages should be available if the learner has trouble with entering a response.

LESSON DESIGN

The lesson design for tutorials involves giving directions to the learner, writing instructional statements and examples, writing teaching questions, and designing linear or branching responses. If you wish to be able to follow the learner's progress through the lesson you may also incorporate a tracking program in the lesson design.

1. Directions. The directions for the tutorial are given so the learner will know how the lesson is designed and what is expected (Fig. 8–2). Inform the learners that if they answer the teaching question correctly they will move on to the next part of the lesson. Also explain that if the question is not answered correctly they have a choice of going back to the same instruction, of trying another instruction with different examples (if this is how your lesson is designed) or of continuing on to the next part of the lesson (if you have designed this type of learner control). Also explain how to enter a response.

Lesson purpose, goal, and objectives can be included in the directions if they were not included in a previous screen. Pretests and posttests may be used with tutorials. If a tracking system is used, tell the learner how the information will be used.

2. Instructional Statements, Examples, and Non Examples. The first part of each section of the tutorial contains instructional statements (Fig. 8–3). Instructional statements should be short, accurate, and clear. Because instructional statements build on each other be certain that the sequence follows your task analysis. Examples are used to explicate the instructional statement (Fig. 8–4). They can precede or follow the instructional statement (Chap. 3). Non examples (Fig. 8–5) can also be used to clarify the instruction.

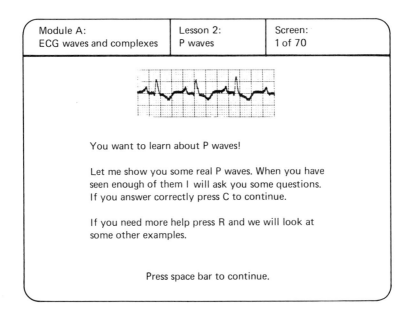

You want to learn about P waves!

Let me show you some real P waves. When you have seen enough of them I will ask you some questions. If you answer correctly press C to continue.

If you need more help press R and we will look at some other examples.

Press space bar to continue.

Figure 8-2. Direction screen for a tutorial.

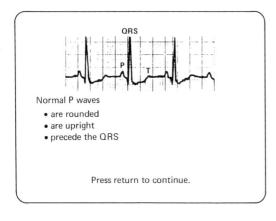

Normal P waves
- are rounded
- are upright
- precede the QRS

Press return to continue.

Figure 8-3. Instructional statement.

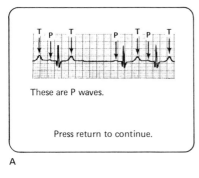

These are P waves.

Press return to continue.

A

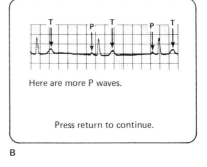

Here are more P waves.

Press return to continue.

B

Figure 8-4. Examples (**A** and **B**).

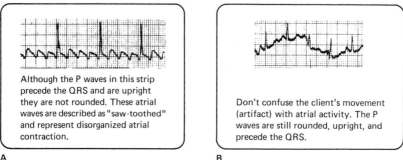

Although the P waves in this strip precede the QRS and are upright they are not rounded. These atrial waves are described as "saw-toothed" and represent disorganized atrial contraction.

Don't confuse the client's movement (artifact) with atrial activity. The P waves are still rounded, upright, and precede the QRS.

A   B

Figure 8-5. Non examples (**A** and **B**).

- Reflect on previous methods of teaching the content of the tutorial for ideas on what type of examples to give.

3. Teaching Questions. The next phase of the tutorial is the interaction or teaching question (Fig. 8–6). Here you ask the student to perform a task (identify the P wave, calculate a drug dose) or answer a question. Questions should be used to validate learning or stimulate discovery and can be short answer, fill-in-the-blank, or multiple choice. Teaching questions must be clear, related to the instruction, and at the appropriate level of the domain of the objective.

- Avoid questions that confuse the student or for which there can be several answers.
- Variety in question design averts boredom.

4. Response. The fourth component of the tutorial is the learner's response to the question.

- The type of question will, of course, determine the type of response and will afford the opportunity to interact with the instruction.

5. Feedback. Feedback follows each question and is given for correct (Fig. 8–7) as well as incorrect responses (Fig. 8–8). Design feedback for each question as you write it. Also indicate clearly where branching occurs if you develop remediation for incorrect responses.

6. Tracking. It is possible to code the lesson so you can follow the student's progress through the tutorial. This information is useful to you in revising the lesson because you can determine which instructional statements and examples are not clear to the learner. Tracking also pro-

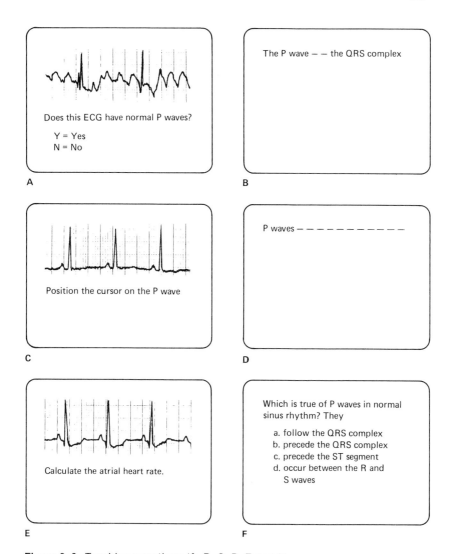

Figure 8-6. Teaching questions (**A, B, C, D, E** and **F**).

vides diagnostic information about the learner and can be used later for writing a learning prescription for a given student.

TRYOUT, REVISION, AND USE

To complete the development cycle for a tutorial you will try out the first draft, and revise as necessary before coding the lesson for computer use. As you use the tutorial you will gather additional information about les-

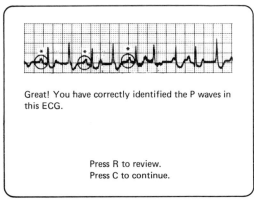

Great! You have correctly identified the P waves in this ECG.

Press R to review.
Press C to continue.

Figure 8-7. Learner response is correct; feedback given visually and verbally. All P waves show inverse video for correct response.

*All P waves show inverse video for correct response.

son validity and reliability. Since the tutorial was developed to meet an instructional need, evaluation should also indicate that the CAI tutorial was useful.

SUMMARY

Tutorials are an exciting way to use the computer to provide individualized and replicable instruction. Tutorials can be designed in a linear mode to direct all learners through the same instruction and examples or in a branched mode which maximizes the capacity of the computer as a medium of individualized instruction. Tutorials are time consuming to develop but save instructional time when sufficient numbers of students use the lesson. In designing any instruction it is necessary to follow an instructional development process that directs you to formulate the

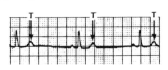

You have identified the T wave. The P wave precedes the QRS. Look again at the P wave in this strip.

Figure 8-8. Learner response is incorrect. Feedback compares learner's incorrect response to correct response.

product, write instructional specifications, design the lesson, and evaluate learning outcomes while trying, revising, and using the tutorial.

The lesson design for a tutorial involves giving directions, preparing instructional statements and examples, writing teaching questions, and anticipating responses, giving feedback to each response and branching to remediation as necessary. A checklist for designing a tutorial is presented at the end of this chapter to give direction as you develop your own tutorial.

CHECKLIST: DESIGNING TUTORIALS

Product formulation:
1. Development time allocated (100 to 150 hours) ____
2. Subject matter expert, instructional developer, programmer (or authoring tool) available ____
3. Outline developed
   a. Instructional statements ____
   b. Examples, non examples ____
   c. Teaching questions ____
   d. Remedial statements, examples, questions ____

Instructional specifications:
1. Needs analysis
   a. Curriculum need ____
   b. Need for individualized instruction ____
   c. Sufficient users ____
2. Learner analysis
   a. Current knowledge ____
   b. Typical mistakes, misunderstanding of content ____
3. Task analysis
   a. Content ____
   b. Sequence ____
4. Purpose, goals, objectives
   a. Relevant ____
   b. Clear ____
5. Tutorial designed using teaching–learning principles
   a. Sequence includes instruction examples, questions, learner response, feedback, remediation ____
   b. Interaction appropriate to task ____

    c. Feedback used to inform learner or coach to correct
      response   _____
    d. Learner has control of amount and sequence of in-
      struction, remediation is optional   _____

Screen design:

  1. Text displayed attractively   _____
  2. Graphics support instruction   _____
  3. Error messages available   _____

Lesson design:

  1. Directions
    a. Progress/remediation explained   _____
    b. Response entry directions given   _____
  2. Instructional statements/examples
    a. Clear   _____
    b. Logical order   _____
    c. Sufficient examples   _____
    d. Choice in number of examples   _____
  3. Teaching questions
    a. Validate learning   _____
    b. Stimulate discovery   _____
    c. Relate to instruction   _____
  4. Learner's response easily accepted   _____
  5. Feedback written for each question   _____
  6. Tracking mechanism available if needed to diagnose
    learner problem areas   _____

Tryout, revision and use:

  1. Tryout
    a. Learner   _____
    b. Subject matter expert   _____
    c. Language expert   _____
  2. Tutorial revised before use   _____
  3. Instructor and student manuals written   _____
  4. Program documentation written   _____
  5. Use meets instructional needs   _____

REFERENCES

Schmidt, M., & Lease, B. (1984). A design for the development of a computer assisted instruction tutorial module. *Computers in Nursing, 2,* 136–142.

Tennyson, R., & Buttry, T. (1980). Advisement and management strategies as design variables in computer-assisted instruction. *Educational Communications and Technology Journal, 28,* 169–176.

Additional Readings

Bork, A. (1980). Preparing student-computer dialogues: Advice to teachers. In R. Taylor (Ed.), *The computer in the school: Tutor, tool, tutee.* New York: Teachers College Press, pp. 15–52.

Gallagher, J. (1981). The effectiveness of man–machine tutorial dialogue for teaching attribute blocks problem-solving skills with an artificial intelligence CAI system. *Instructional Science, 10,* 297–332.

Gentner, D. (1979). Toward an intelligent computer tutor. In H. O'Neil (Ed.), *Procedures for instructional systems development.* New York: Academic Press.

Levine, D., & Wiener, E. (1975). Let the computer teach it. *American Journal of Nursing, 75,* 1300–1302.

Van Dongen, C., & Van Dongen, W. (1984). Using microcomputers to teach psychopharmacology. *Journal of Nursing Education, 23,* 259–260.

9

Designing Simulations

Simulations or representations of the real world are an exciting instructional use of the computer where the learner can exercise judgment and make decisions. After reading this chapter you will be able to select a topic for a simulation, prepare an overview and blueprint, as well as design the simulation lesson. You will also be able to incorporate pre-simulation and debriefing activities as you use a simulation with your students.

SIMULATIONS

Simulations are hypothetical situations that imitate a real physical or social setting. The learner participates in the hypothetical situation by gathering data and choosing actions which in turn require subsequent decisions and actions. Simulations are active learning environments and provide the learner with the opportunity to manipulate variables or discover problem-solving approaches without incurring danger, expense, time, or untoward effects upon real-world clients or work settings.

Design Concept

Simulations consist of a scenario, data gathering, and management options, and bridges to subsequent data gathering and management options as the simulation unfolds (Fig. 9-1). The scenario delineates the practice setting and problem to be solved. Data gathering options are used to provide the learner with an opportunity to assess the client or gather data as the problem evolves while management options provide choices for problem solutions. The simulation terminates when the learner solves the problem (or initiates a hazardous action).

Each simulation has an optimal problem solution (optimal path) and several less optimal or even hazardous problem solutions (Fig. 9-1). The simulation can be linear or branching. In a linear design all students follow the same path. In branching designs, however, there are a variety of courses of action, some of which solve the problem efficiently and effectively, and others which may simply waste time or are dangerous and can cause a premature end to the hypothetical situation. A combination of linear and branching paths is used in most simulations.

Instructional Use

Simulations teach at higher cognitive levels of application, analysis, and synthesis. They are, therefore, used after other instruction such as lectures, assigned readings, CAI tutorial, or drill and practice which establish the content base on which the simulation builds. They are best used

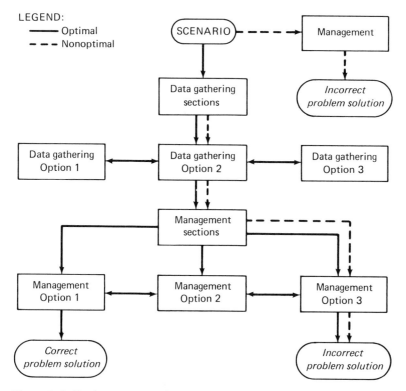

Figure 9-1. Design concept: simulation.

to reinforce learning of facts, concepts, principles, and to apply process skills.

Simulations provide a safe learning environment for clinical instruction because decisions and actions can be made without real-world consequences. Time is compressed, allowing the learner to determine actions and evaluate outcomes without time lags common to actual client care.

Simulations are also used for clinical or classroom evaluation (Sweeney, 1982; Kolb & Schugart, 1984). They provide a semblance of the real world as well as constant variables against which all students can be evaluated.

PRODUCT FORMULATION

Simulations are elaborate instructional environments and require careful planning to create replications of problems and solutions. Resources of time and personnel should be available for designing simulations.

Time, Money, and Resources

Developing simulations is the most complex and time-consuming type of
CAI to develop. A computer programmer or authoring system should be
identified at the outset so the program can be coded for the computer.
Persons with previous experience designing simulations are also helpful
allies.

- A project team is usually more effective in developing simulations; ideas are generated easily in a close working group.
- A project team allows members to give support to each other and
  keeps forward momentum in the project.
- Allocate generous blocks of time to work on the simulation. Once
  the ideas start to flow it's hard to stop.
- Simulations can take up to 250 hours of development time for a
  1 hour simulation.

Outline

Before embarking on writing a simulation you must first select a topic
and write an outline. This may be the most time-consuming part of the
project. Two types of outlines are used to organize computer simulations. One is an overview, the other is a flowchart.

Topic Selection. Topics used for simulations must have a correspondence to reality and a problem-solving component that involve data gathering, data processing, decision making, and evaluation. Ideal topics are
those that involve several stages of data gathering and problem management and in which the outcome is affected by the learner's decisions.
The topic must also encourage the learner to use previously learned
knowledge, attitudes, or skills.

Keep the topic short and limited. This is imperative when designing
your first simulation. It is tempting to select a topic that has a complex
data base and a variety of decisions that can be made. Resist this temptation and confine the topic to its simplest elements.

- Limit details of the topic or it will quickly get out of hand.
- Balance reality with complexity.
- Limit the topic to a single problem. A client with diabetes mellitus, an amputated leg, a myocardial infarction, high anxiety, im-
  paired elimination, and knowledge deficits may be a bit
  complicated for your first simulation!
- Keep the setting for the simulation simple. Even though the real
  world is complex you do not need to elaborate or incorporate those
  details.

Overview. The simulation overview is a series of narrative statements that describes the optimal and non optimal sequences of problem solution (Fig. 9–2). The overview is, in essence, the plot of the simulation. The overview provides direction for more detailed development of the simulation.

Blueprint. The blueprint is a flowchart showing the scenario, data collection, and management options for optimal and non optimal paths (Fig. 9–3). Because the simulation becomes complex as each step of the process unfolds you will frequently refer to the blueprint for orientation.

During lesson design you will probably have additional ideas about how the simulation could evolve. Although the blueprint is a guideline, you may need to go back and adjust the blueprint as the simulation develops.

- The blueprint can be used as a marketing tool to quickly show others the framework of the simulation.
- The blueprint can be used in the documentation or teacher's and learner's guides to the simulation to show the outcomes of the optimal and non optimal paths.
- Once you develop an outline for one topic, the next outline is easier. When developing several try to find a frame for all and spend development time on the framework.

The simulation opens with a nurse, newly employed in a large hospital, requesting time off work to attend a wedding.

The nurse must decide which information about the organizational structure is needed to request time off. The policy manual and procedure manual are essential choices.

If the nurse seeks information only from the personnel director, the policy manual or hospital philosophy he or she will not obtain sufficient information and the request for time off will not be processed.

When the nurse examines the procedure and policy manuals the nurse is given more information about routing the request.

Information given by the Director of Nurses, evening supervisor, or clinical charge nurse is inaccurate and thwarts the request.

Upon viewing the organizational chart the nurse realizes the request must go to the unit manager and the nurse can have the time off if he or she finds a replacement. The choice of an LPN is inappropriate; a memo to the personnel director does not follow the lines of command indicated in the procedure and the request is denied.

The successful problem solution requires the nurse to find a registered nurse to work during the requested time off. The central nursing staffing office is notified and the request is granted.

Figure 9–2. Simulation overview.

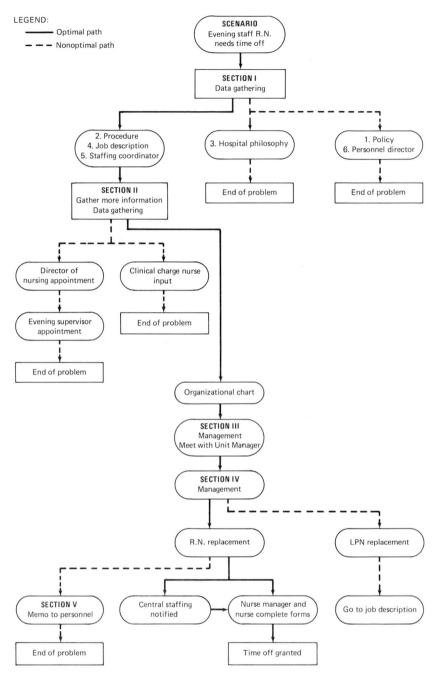

Figure 9-3. Blueprint. (From Billings, D., Keating, T., & Soja, M. (1985). Requesting time off: A nursing management simulation. Unpublished simulation. Indiana University, School of Nursing, Indianapolis Ind., with permission.)

INSTRUCTIONAL SPECIFICATIONS

Instructional specifications are written to guide development of the simulation. They include needs analysis, learner analysis, task analysis, purpose, goals, and objectives, and teaching–learning principles.

Needs Analysis

Simulations meet curriculum and learner needs to teach a process and improve problem-solving skills and hierarchical thinking (Peterson, 1984). Simulations also meet needs for clinical experience because students can practice clinical judgments without risk to the client. Simulations meet needs where clinical experiences are limited because the same simulated clinical experience can be offered to all students. In the classroom, simulations meet the needs for gaining the learner's attention and generating enthusiasm.

Learner Analysis

Simulations are developed for a specific learner group. Learner analysis is used to determine that the learner is familiar with the process being simulated and has the necessary skills to solve the problem.

If the learner is a beginning student with little clinical practice the setting of the simulation should be simple and the data needed to be collected should be minimal. If on the other hand, the learner is an experienced health professional and the simulation is being used for orientation, staff development, or continuing education, the simulation can be as complex as the work environment. Data used to solve the problem should be complex and require the learner to differentiate significant and insignificant data, effective and ineffective actions.

Learners solve problems in a variety of ways. These differences are more clearly noted between novices and experts (Benner, 1982). Inexperienced health professionals solve problems by gathering small bits of information and proceeding forward to solve a problem, while those with experience deal with large data bases, sift and sort for clues, and use a global approach to problem solving. These learner differences should be kept in mind while designing simulations, particularly since the designer is likely to be an expert with global problem-solving abilities and the learner using the simulation may be a novice.

Task Analysis

Simulations are problem-solving tasks, and a task analysis is used to identify and sequence each step of the process. Performing a task analysis (Chap. 3) is crucial in simulations because an omission or incorrect sequence may confuse the learner.

Purpose, Goals, and Objectives

The purpose of simulations is to provide the learner with an opportunity to solve a problem, and the goal of instruction is for the student to learn or discover the optimal problem solution. Objectives are written at higher levels in the learning taxonomy and typically include application or analysis. The learner should always be informed of the purpose, goals, and objectives of the simulation.

Teaching–Learning Principles

Teaching–learning principles are selected to encourage the learner to use problem-solving skills. Sequence, feedback, and motivation are therefore important elements in designing simulations.

Sequence. The instructional sequence of the simulation (Chap. 4) is questions, learner response, and consequences (information or results). Because a simulation involves application of previously learned content, instructional statements are not used in this strategy. The sequence of the simulation follows the problem-solving steps identified through task analysis. Although the sequence in the optimal path moves in a forward direction the branches of non optimal paths may vary.

Feedback. Feedback in simulations, unlike that in tutorials or drill and practice lessons, is a response to a request for data or a response to a health care action or management strategy. The feedback is not corrective and unless learners deduce they have made an incorrect choice, they are not routed to remediation or given a second attempt to obtain the correct response.

Feedback about the success (or lack of success) in problem solving is reserved for the end of the simulation. Feedback here is given as a score and as a component of the debriefing that occurs after each simulation.

- Showing learners the blueprint so they can see an overview may be helpful feedback after the simulation.

Motivation. Simulations should be motivating. They should be short enough to hold the learner's attention and long enough to challenge. Motivation is heightened when choices and results are varied. If the learner can "second guess" the next move, he or she may try non optimal paths to keep the lesson interesting. At the same time, non optimal paths should be plausible but not more exciting than the optimal path. The action pace of the simulation can be varied and should give learners a sense of accomplishment as they progress through the lesson. Motivation can also be enhanced by turning the simulation into a game by introducing competition or time limits.

SCREEN DESIGN

The screen design for simulations can contribute to developing the "plot." Graphics can be used, for example, to show the results of actions such as an infusion of intravenous fluid or display data such as vital signs or ECG changes. Graphics in non optimal paths, however, should not be so exciting that they entice the learner to follow that course of action.

If large amounts of information are used in data collection it may be advisable to have the information available in a workbook off screen. Client records, vital signs charts, and lab values may be more appropriately given in a workbook. If the learner is to remember the data for later use, give directions to make notes as needed. If the information is to be referred to again, it will be necessary to design the program so that data screens can be accessed when needed.

- Adjunct materials such as videotapes, slides, charts, or kardexes can be used to create interest and display data. Include these in the storyboard as screen designs.

LESSON DESIGN

The overview and blueprint prepared earlier are used now for lesson development. Using the flowchart or storyboard, you will give flesh to the skeleton of the blueprint.

- A flowchart can be drawn on used computer print paper. The entire lesson can be developed from the attached pages.
- If you are using 5″ × 8″ cards for a storyboard be sure to carefully label connectors and branches as you can become confused about where paths are leading.

1. Directions. The directions for the learner using the simulation are significant if the learner has never used a simulation before. The fact that there is no one correct response, but rather the learner is choosing optimal actions must be made clear (Fig. 9–4). Inform the learner that

---

DIRECTIONS

This simulation involves a situation that you would encounter in a clinical setting. The setting and other necessary information are described in the scenario which will be displayed on the third screen.

You will be presented with alternatives for data gathering and management decisions. According to the alternatives you select, the results of the data gathering or the outcome of the management decision will be displayed on the screen. You will then be presented with another set of pertinent alternatives until the problem is solved.

A

As you progress through the simulation think in terms of helpful, neutral, or harmful actions, not those that are just right or wrong. You need to gather enough information but not waste time with unnecessary information.

At each decision point you will be provided with directions. The directions will inform you if you may select more than one alternative. Be sure to read the directions carefully.

Each section is scored to reflect information gathering and management decisions. The object of this simulation is to solve the problem in the most effective and efficient way. Your score will be reported at the end of the simulation.

B

Figure 9-4. Directions for simulations (**A** and **B**).

information is given after each data collection or management choice and that subsequent decisions should be based on that information. If the simulation is scored, indicate to the learner that the score will be reported at the end of the simulation.

- The purpose, goals, and objectives should accompany or precede the directions.
- Although directions appear early in the simulation you may find them easier to write after you have developed the simulation.

2. Scenario. The scenario, or opening scene, sets the stage for events to follow by explaining the task to be accomplished, the role of the learner, the setting in which the action takes place, the aspects of time and resources, and any other necessary information about the problem (Fig. 9-5). Irrelevant information should also be included in the scenario, establishing that the learner can sort significant and insignificant data at the outset. The scenario is usually presented on screen but could be presented in a videotape (videodisk), client record, slides, audiotape, or in a workbook.

The scenario establishes the *task* the learner is to accomplish. The task may involve using a specific process, such as the nursing process, or a component of a process, such as making a diagnosis or implementing a care plan, or making a staffing assignment for a group of clients. The task should be very clear to the learner. If time limits are imposed for task completion these should also be known to the learner.

The *role* the learner is to play in the simulation is also explained in the scenario. For instance, the learner may be a student, a nurse, a physician, a respiratory therapist, a manager, or a person who is newly diagnosed with diabetes mellitus and requiring insulin. The learner is informed of the level of expertise expected. Roles could be explained by a job description.

Simulations mimic real settings, and the scenario is used to give the learner information about the *setting* in which the action will take place. Descriptions of settings can include physical descriptions, staffing patterns, kinds of equipment available, or location. The setting should be as close to reality as possible.

All real-life settings have *limits* and *constraints*. These need to be identified to the learner if they have an impact on the problem. Constraints can include information that the client can only have pain medication every 3 hours or that one nurse has called in sick and staffing patterns are changed.

- When developing the scenario, avoid using information that gives unintended cues.

SCENARIO

ROLE: You have been employed as an R.N. on a hospital unit for 6 months as a team leader on the evening shift. It is now February 16. Your best friend, who lives 2,000 miles away, has requested that you be an attendant at her wedding on June 6.

TASK: You would like to attend the wedding but you will need to request 5 days off work so you can get there for the rehearsal and allow enough time for travel. You will need to determine how you can have the time off.

A

CONSTRAINTS: At the hospital where you work the staffing plan is made in the central staffing office. The schedule is posted through June. The rotation plan is 5, 8-hour days with 2 days off each week.

SETTING: The nursing unit where you are the team leader has 30 beds. There are 3 teams, staffed with a team leader and 2 or 3 team members.

EXTRANEOUS INFORMATION: The unit manager on this unit tends to be "authoritarian", but you decide to risk her displeasure because you really want to be in the wedding.

B

Figure 9-5. Scenario (**A** and **B**).

- Extraneous information in the scenario should be believable.
- Keep the scenario simple, as the learner might be overwhelmed with the role and setting before even starting.
- Do not include too much information in the scenario; save it for the learners to gather themselves as the simulation unfolds.

3. Sections. The sections that follow the scenario are used to require the learner to gather data and manage the problem. Each section has option statements and bridging statements.

The *option statement* provides the learner with a choice about gathering information or choosing a course of action. Options are constructed to reflect a range of choices from those that are essential or helpful to those that are harmful or even dangerous (Fig. 9–6).

Option statements either request the student to gather data or initiate action or manage a problem. *Data gathering statements* direct the learner to make assessments or gather information. The information may be obtained from the client, records (history, client chart, care plans, kardex), physical examination, organizational charts, the client's family, or other health care workers. Data gathering option statements can direct the learner to essential, neutral, or harmful (unnecessary) data.

Option statements about *actions* or management ask the learner to choose between several courses of action. The action may be to gather data, develop a plan, implement or evaluate care. Again, these options range from essential to harmful.

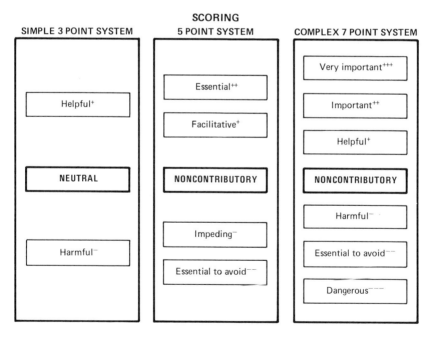

Figure 9-6. Ranges of option statements for data gathering and management options to be used in scoring simulation. (Adapted from McGuire, C., Solomon, L., & Bashook, P. (1975). Construction and use of written simulations. Cleveland, Ohio: Psychological Corporation, with permission.)

When the learner makes a choice of one (or more than one if needed) option, the data or outcome are revealed on the screen. These data or results are now the source of subsequent data collection or actions. Bridging statements are used to direct the learner to the next section.

Bridging statements tie the results of option statements to the next sequence of events by giving instructions to move from section to section. Bridges may be linear or branched (Fig. 9-7). Their use depends on the learner's choice of option statements and events within the simulation.

In *linear* programs all learners follow the same path; there is no branching to alternative paths. Linear programs are often used in the beginning of the simulation to start all learners toward problem solution or at the end of the simulation when choices for action are limited.

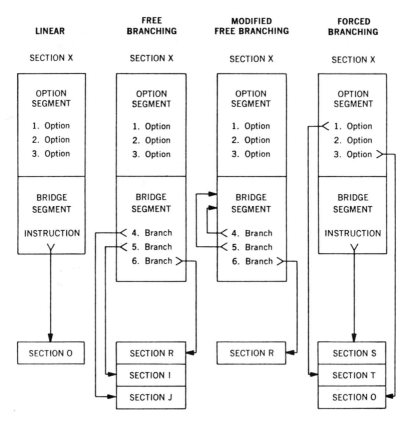

Figure 9-7. Schematic representation of four bridging techniques. (From McGuire, C., Solomon, L., & Bashook, P. (1975). Construction and use of written simulations. Cleveland, Ohio: Psychological Corporation, with permission.)

Branching programs, on the other hand, provide alternative courses of action, which can be essential, neutral, or harmful. Branching is used to vary the process by which the student solves the problem or completes the task. Branches are the essence of the simulation and can be complicated as learners choose inappropriate paths.

There are three types of branching statements: free choice, forced choice, and modified free choice (McGuire, et al., 1975) (Fig. 9-7). In *free choice branching* the learner decides which course to take. The learner's own problem-solving skills dictate the route to problem solution.

Free choice branching can be controlled by *forced choice branching* which directs the learner to the next section. Here there is only one option. Forced choice branching is used when the next course of action is clear, or to bring errant students back toward the optimal path.

Modified free choice branching provides the learner with limited choices. This type of branching is used to assure forward progress in the simulation or to limit dangerous action at some point in the simulation.

- All four types of bridges are used in most simulations.
- One hour of simulation may use more than 250 option statements.

4. Optimal Path. The optimal path reflects the best way to solve the problem using appropriate data gathering strategies and making wise management decisions. After writing the scenario, you can use option statements and bridges to develop the optimal path. Follow your overview and blueprint to be certain each step of the simulation is included.

- Writing the optimal path first establishes direction for the remainder of the simulation.
- Using a flowchart enables you to see the length and levels of your optimal path.
- If you are using a storyboard, place the cards on a long table or bulletin board so you can see the extent of the optimal path for problem solution.

5. Non Optimal Path. Non optimal paths are more easily developed after establishing the optimal path. Return now to each section and create options for data gathering and management that are neutral or harmful. Non optimal paths should be plausible, however, and conform to the parameters established in the scenario.

Non optimal paths can lead to unsafe or harmful problem solutions and early termination of the simulation. These paths do correspond to reality (giving mismatched blood, for example, can cause death) but create an opportunity for further teaching and learning.

- Ideas for non optimal paths often come from experience with the target audience. Learners often do gather irrelevant data or select inappropriate courses of action. Use these examples for non optimal path development.
- When rerouting the learner back to the optimal path, use bridging statements that fill in the story to date. (If the learner has missed a part of the optimal path some information may be missing that is needed later.)
- Keep non optimal paths simple. The learner can benefit from a succinct mistake.

6. Scoring. Once the entire simulation is developed, a scoring system must be established. A scoring system is used to give learners feedback about their proficiency with problem solution, to assign a grade, or to diagnose a learning problem. The scores should therefore reflect the significance of actions and decisions at each point of the simulation.

In a simple scoring system, weight is given to actions that are essential, neutral, or harmful, with more weight or positive scores given to essential action. In more elaborate systems the actions can be weighted using a 5- or 7-point scale (Fig. 9-6) to reflect the range of actions and decisions and their seriousness.

Scoring systems can be developed using positive numbers ($+1$ to $+5$, etc.) or positive and negative numbers (-5 to $+5$, etc.). A positive number system makes addition and subtraction easier, while using positive and negative numbers keeps the numbers smaller. Either system should reflect safe practice, however.

After deciding on the scoring system, go through the optimal path and score it first. This should result in the highest possible score and represent essential actions at each section. Next, score the non optimal paths. These, of course, should yield a lower score. If branching is sophisticated it is possible for non optimal paths to have a high score because the learner has made many choices and actions. If your non optimal path yields a higher score, adjust the scoring by decreasing the scores for non optimal actions or by giving more weight to the optimal path.

- Keep scoring simple in your first simulations.
- Check and double check scoring; mistakes are easy to make.
- Follow all possible routes to verify scoring.
- Proficiency levels can be determined from the range of scores. Some students enjoy knowing they were "above average," or gave "very safe care!"

TRYOUT, REVISION, AND USE

Simulations require rigorous tryout and revision before they are ready for use. In spite of the temptation to use them immediately, you will have a better simulation if you follow the tryout and revision procedures suggested below.

Tryout

The flowchart or storyboard can be used for the first tryout of your simulation. Each member of the design team should go through the simulation and edit or correct errors. Check the simulation against the overview and blueprint to assure a match. Follow each branch to its conclusion and correct or create bridging statements as needed.

Because the simulation is a representative of reality ask someone who experiences the reality to use the simulation. Hopefully, this subject matter expert will concur with your optimal path and find non optimal paths realistic. Differences of opinion should be resolved before use with learners.

Next, recruit several people from the target audience to use the simulation. Observe the learners as they go through the simulation and ask their rationale for selecting one option statement instead of another. Here you will discover if the learner can solve the problem, as well as obtain ideas for revising non optimal paths. If necessary, coach the learner through optimal and non optimal paths to discover the reasoning behind choices.

Finally, ask a colleague with strong writing skills to read the simulation for clarity of directions and correct word use. Jargon and confusing terms should be removed.

Revision

After obtaining suggestions from subject matter experts, learners, and grammarians you are ready to revise the simulation. If possible, try the first revision of the simulation on another group of learners. Use this draft in the setting in which it will be ultimately used if at all possible.

When resources permit, you can convert the draft into a written simulation, instructing the learner to turn to pages, instead of screen displays. Data from this use of the simulation can be helpful in establishing simulation reliability and give you yet another chance to obtain ideas for revision before committing the lesson to the computer.

When the lesson is as well designed as possible, you are ready to code the problem using a programming language or authoring system. The next revision cycle follows as colleagues and learners use the computer version. Again, follow optimal and non optimal paths to their conclusion. The scoring system should also pass a final check. Problems discovered at this stage necessitate reprogramming or adjusting screen design.

The instructor's manual, student's manual, adjunct materials, and program documentation are written after the final program revision. The final tryout is conducted with a group of instructors and learners who have not been a part of the development process.

Using Simulations

Special procedures are used to enhance the instructional effectiveness of simulations. These include presimulation activities and postsimulation activities, or debriefing.

Presimulation Activities. Before using a simulation with learners it is important to verify learner knowledge and skill. This can be accomplished with an entry test or review if needed. Simulations are therefore usually used after the content or skill has been mastered.

Debriefing. After the student has used the simulation a mechanism must be established for giving the learner feedback about his or her performance and for discussing the rationale for each path to problem solution. Debriefing is best conducted immediately after the learner has used the simulation.

Debriefing can take place in several ways. One way is to include debriefing in the lesson where the learner does it independently on the computer at the conclusion of the simulation. The learner is given the score, the rationale is explained for the course of action the individual learner selected, and suggestions are given to the learner for further study.

Debriefing can also be managed without the computer by using a student workbook. The rationale for all choices is explained, and the blueprint can be used to show the learner the sequence of events. Discussion questions are used to stimulate the learner to analyze or synthesize learning.

Group discussion is another way of holding a debriefing session. Here divergent opinions and peer suggestions facilitate learning. Expert clinicians can also be invited to support the rationale for problem solution and compare and contrast reality and simulation.

SUMMARY

Simulations are a versatile instructional strategy used for teaching and evaluating. They are at the same time one of the most complicated types of CAI lessons to develop and use. It is important therefore to begin formulating the simulation by assuring adequate resources and preparing an overview and blueprint. Instructional specifications are written to establish need, determine learner competence, analyze the task being simulated, state purpose, goals, objectives, and use appropriate teaching-learning principles. The screen design should contribute to the vitality of the simulation, but it may be necessary to place large data sources in a workbook to decrease learner memory load.

The lesson design must include directions, the scenario, data gathering and data management sections with options and bridges to the next section, and the optimal path and other paths that are time wasting or even harmful. The scoring of a simulation gives the learner feedback about the effectiveness of actions during the simulation.

The tryout and revision cycle is rigorous when developing simulations. The design team, learners, and subject experts are recruited to try the simulation before final programming. Revisions are common and can be extensive.

When simulations are used the instructor must assure learner readiness and allow time for debriefing afterwards. These can be done in the CAI simulation or in group discussions.

Simulations are powerful teaching-evaluating situations for students. A checklist is included at the end of this chapter to assist you as you develop your own simulation.

CHECKLIST: DESIGNING SIMULATIONS

Product formulation:
1. Development time allocated (100 to 250 hours) _____
2. Programmer (or authoring system) available _____
3. Instructional developer available _____
4. Design team colleagues available _____
5. Topic selected
    a. Is problem solving _____
    b. Represents behavior to be taught/evaluated _____

    c. Represents reality   _____
    d. Has several stages of data gathering and management   _____
  6. Overview written   _____
  7. Blueprint developed
    a. Shows optimal path   _____
    b. Shows non optimal path   _____

Instructional specifications:

  1. Needs analysis
    a. Needs for problem-solving skills identified   _____
    b. Needs for clinical skills identified   _____
  2. Learner analysis
    a. Content presented before simulation used   _____
    b. Learner experience matches expectations of simulation   _____
    c. Learner problem-solving capability (novice vs. expert) identified   _____
  3. Task analysis
    a. Simulation based on task or process   _____
    b. Sequence of simulation follows process   _____
  4. Purpose, goals, objectives
    a. Purpose matches reality   _____
    b. Objectives written for application or analysis   _____
  5. Simulation designed using teaching–learning principles
    a. Sequence follows task analysis   _____
    b. Feedback is informational   _____
    c. Feedback about results (score) given at end of simulation   _____
    d. Option statements are varied   _____
    e. Non optimal paths are less exciting than optimal path   _____
    f. Non optimal paths are plausible   _____

Screen design:

  1. Graphics used appropriately   _____
  2. Data displayed consistently on screen   _____
  3. Large data bases displayed in workbook   _____
  4. Paper and pencil provided for recording data, calculation, etc.   _____
  5. Adjuncts (videotape, kardex, slides) contribute to scenario as needed   _____

Lesson design:

1. Directions explain process of choosing optimal options
   of data collection or management
   a. Explain scoring _____
   b. How to enter data _____
2. The scenario includes:
   a. Task _____
   b. Role _____
   c. Setting _____
   d. Limits and constraints _____
   e. Extraneous information _____
3. Option statements offer realistic choices
   a. Essential _____
   b. Neutral _____
   c. Harmful _____
4. Bridging statements give instructions to move learner
   from one section to the next _____
5. Bridging statements for non optimal paths update
   learner about problem progress _____
6. Optimal path reflects correct problem solution _____
7. Non optimal paths are realistic _____
8. Scoring reflects safe nursing practice _____

Tryout, revision, and use:

1. Tryout of storyboard draft includes:
   a. Learner _____
   b. Subject matter expert _____
   c. Design team _____
   d. Language expert _____
2. Simulation revised before use
   a. Tryout with target audience _____
   b. Instructor/student manuals developed _____
   c. Program documentation written _____
3. Use includes:
   a. Presimulation activities to verify knowledge or skill _____
   b. Debriefing _____

REFERENCES

Benner, P. (1982). From novice to expert. *American Journal of Nursing, 82,* 402–407.

Kolb, S., & Shugart, E. (1984). Evaluation: Is simulation the answer? *Journal of Nursing Education, 23*, 84–86.
McGuire, C., Solomon, L., & Bashook, P. (1975). Construction and use of written simulations. Cleveland, Ohio: Psychological Corporation.
Peterson, N. (1984). Designing a simulated laboratory. *Byte, 9*(6), 287–296.
Sweeney, M. A., et al. (1982). Development of a computer simulation. *Journal of Nursing Education, 21*(9), 28–38.

Additional Readings

Bashook, P. (1982). Written simulations: From paper format to computer format and beyond. *National Society for Performance and Instruction Journal, 11*, 12–15.
Clark, C. (1976). Simulation gaming: A new teaching strategy in nursing education. *Nurse Educator, 1*(4), 4–9.
Cooper, S. (1979). Methods of teaching-revisited games and simulation. *Journal of Continuing Education in Nursing, 10*(5), 14.
Duke, R. (1975). Public policy applications: Using gaming-simulations for problem exploration and decision-making. In C. Greenflat & R. Duke (Eds.), *Gaming-simulation: Rationale, design and application*. New York: Wiley.
Duraiswamy, N., Welton, R., & Reisman, A. (1981). Using computer simulation to predict ICU staffing needs. *Journal of Nursing Administration, 11*(2), 39–44.
Feldman, J., & Heindert, M. (1977). Determining nursing policies by use of the nursing home simulation model. *Journal of Nursing Administration, 7*(4), 35–41.
Feldt, A., & Goodman, I. (1975). Observations on the design of simulations and games. In C. Greenflat & R. Duke (Eds.), *Gaming-simulation: Rationale, design and application*. New York: Wiley.
Grobe, S. (1984). Computer assisted instruction, an alternative. *Computers in Nursing, 2*, 92–97.
Laszlo, S., & McKenzie, J. (1979). The use of a simulation game in training hospital staff about patient rights. *Journal of Continuing Education in Nursing, 10*(5), 30–36.
Miller, M. (1984). The use of simulations in training programs: A review. *Educational Technology, 24*(11), 39–42.
Rowe, N. C. (1984). Some rules for good simulations. In D. Walker & R. Hess, (Eds.), *Instructional software: Principles and perspectives for design and use*. Belmont, Calif.: Wadsworth.
Schleutermann, J., Holzemer, W., & Farrard, L. (1983). An evaluation of paper-and-pencil and computer-assisted simulations. *Journal of Nursing Education, 22*, 315–323.
Stevens, A., & Roberts, B. (1983). Quantitative and qualitative simulation in computer based training. *Journal of Computer-Based Instruction, 10*(182), 16–19.
Thiagarajan, S., & Stolovitch, H. (1978). *Instructional simulation games*. Englewood Cliffs, N. J.: Educational Technology Publications.
Ulione, M. S. (1983). Simulation gaming in nursing education. *Journal of Nursing Education, 22*, 349–351.

10

Designing Tests

Tests are another way to use the computer to maximize instruction and evaluation. In this chapter you will learn to differentiate types of tests and identify advantages of using computerized tests. You will also learn how to develop a computer test by formulating the product, writing instructional specifications, designing the test, and completing the tryout, revision, and use cycle.

TESTS

Tests are used to determine the learner's knowledge before, during, and after instruction. Standardized tests can also be used to diagnose learner abilities as compared to others. Standardized computer tests, for example, are used to prepare students for state board licensure examination as well as for certification in clinical practice specialties. Before you design your own test, it is helpful to understand the different types of tests as well as the advantages of using computer testing.

Types of Tests

There are several types of tests used in computer assisted instruction. The most common are pretest/posttest, formative, summative, adaptive, and computer managed.

Pretests and Posttests. Pretests and posttests are used before and after instruction to measure proficiency or mastery according to criteria. Pretests and posttests are parallel forms of the same test. If the learner passes the pretest, he or she can be advanced to the next lesson of study.

Formative Tests. Formative tests are used by the learner and teacher to measure understanding of instruction soon after it is presented. Formative evaluation can include practice examples or a practice test. Feedback is given to the learner about the number of items missed, why the items were missed, and the type of items (content, process) missed. Learners can then be directed (or direct themselves) to review the content that was not understood.

Formative tests are useful when the goal of instruction is mastery. Formative tests are often used after the completion of a module to verify mastery and serve as an entry test into the next module. Formative tests are also used prior to an examination that will be used to assign a grade so the learner can correct errors before grading occurs.

Summative Tests. Summative tests are administered after learning and remediation have occurred. Formative tests may or may not be used to prepare the learner for this test. Here feedback is given at the end of the test and generally only includes a score.

Adaptive Tests. Adaptive tests are individualized as the learner progresses through the test (Kreiztberg, et al., 1984; Weiss, 1979). The selection of the test item is based on the testee's knowledge of a content area at the highest levels. The first question, for example, is obtained from items at higher cognitive levels or representative of content mastery. If, on the other hand, the learner does not answer the first question correctly, items from a lower cognitive level are used. Although adaptive tests are more difficult to construct, this type of testing can decrease testing time. Adaptive tests are useful, therefore, in training programs when it is important for the learner to progress through modules of instruction quickly.

Computer Managed Testing. Computer managed testing (CMT) is a system in which the computer administers, scores, and gives feedback to learners as they progress through instruction. CMT is used with formative evaluation and has the advantage of being self-administered and self-paced. As the learner completes a lesson or module he or she can choose to take a test and, based on the results, proceed to the next lesson. A record is retained for the learner and for the instructor.

Design Concept

The design concept of a test is simple and only includes questions, responses, and a score (Fig. 10-1). The cycle of question and response is continued until the learner has completed the test.

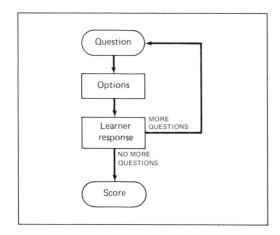

Figure 10-1. Design concept: Test.

Instructional Uses

Computerized testing has several advantages for the teacher and for the learner. Computer tests can be self-administered and self-paced, thereby freeing the teacher for individual instruction instead. The results are immediately available and decisions can be made about further instruction based on test results.

Computerized testing can also be used to prepare students for subsequent course examinations or standardized tests such as the state board licensure examination. Reynolds (1984) finds that using the computer improves situational test-taking skills and decreases test anxiety.

PRODUCT FORMULATION

As with designing any instructional product it is necessary to follow a design sequence to assure attention to all details of test construction. Before developing a computer test it is advisable to allocate time, money, and personnel to the project and develop a test outline.

Time, Money, and Resources

Computer tests are less time consuming than other CAI strategies; a 22-item multiple choice test, for example, can be produced in 25 to 50 hours (Reynolds, 1984). A consultant with testing expertise is a useful addition to your design team and, if needed, should be invited during the product formulation stage.

Outline

The outline for a test includes a statement about the content to be covered, the number of questions to be included, and the time the test will take (if time-limited). Test specifications based on lesson or course content and objectives are determined by task analysis and written at that time.

INSTRUCTIONAL SPECIFICATIONS

Instructional specifications are determined prior to writing the test. Instructional specifications for tests include needs analysis, learner analysis, task analysis, purpose, goals, and objectives, and teaching–learning principles.

Needs Analysis

Needs analysis for a test involves identifying the purpose for the test and its relationship to the lesson or course. The test may be used for verifying learner progress (pretest/posttest, formative evaluation), for measuring the end results of instruction (summative evaluation, posttest), or to determine and assign grades (summative). During needs analysis you should also be certain that the computer is the most efficient and cost-effective way to administer a test.

Learner Analysis

Tests are designed with the learner in mind. You should be aware of the content the learner has mastered and consider the learner's experience with the type of test to be administered. If, for example, the test is to be given to a client, be certain the client is familiar with testing procedures and terms used in the test.

Task Analysis

The table of test specifications (test map) evolves from an analysis of the behavior and content identified in lesson goals and objectives. There are several ways of writing a table of specifications for a test.

One way of making a table of test specifications is to plot a grid of behaviors and content (Brightman, et al., 1984). The behaviors in the domain (cognitive, affective, or psychomotor) to be tested are placed on the horizontal axis in ascending order of difficulty. The content areas to be tested are placed on the vertical axis (Table 10-1). Next, determine

TABLE 10-1. TEST MAP FOR COGNITIVE DOMAIN

Content	Table of Specifications for Managing Acute Pain				
	Knowledge	Compre-hension	Appli-cation	Analysis Synthesis	Evaluation
Definition of acute pain		2			
Assessing client's pain			3		
Planning to relieve pain		2			
Implementing strategies to relieve pain			10		
Evaluating pain relief			3		

how many questions will be asked about the behavior and content. Not all content or all behaviors need to be tested.

Wedman and Stefanich (1984) suggest another approach to test mapping. They identify three main types of content: concepts, principles, and procedures and suggest a table of test specifications for evaluating each of these (Table 10-2). You may wish to construct your test map in this manner if you have similarly identified your content.

Test maps are often published by licensing agencies such as the National Council Licensure Examination for Registered Nurse Licensure (NCLEX). Some faculty (and courseware publishers) use test maps for designing review tests for students who will be taking these types of examinations (Table 10-3).

Purpose, Goals, and Objectives

The purpose, goals, and objectives of instruction should be established prior to constructing a test. Because the test and the objective should match you may wish to check your objectives against the table of specifications to assure a fit.

Teaching-Learning Principles

The pedagogy of testing is different from that of instruction. Of particular concern is the use of feedback, the sequence of instruction, the use of learner control, and the time allocated for testing.

Feedback. Feedback in testing is informational rather than reinforcing. In formative tests the learner is given information that the response is either correct or incorrect. At the conclusion of the test you may choose to inform the learner of content or process errors and provide suggestions for review.

In summative tests the only feedback given to the learner is that the

TABLE 10-2. TEST SPECIFICATIONS FOR CONCEPTS, PRINCIPLES, AND PROCEDURES

Content	How Evaluated
Concept	The learner selects examples from non examples
Principles	The learner applies principle in the way the principle will be used outside the learning situation
Procedure	The learner performs procedure under conditions similar to those outside the learning situation

**TABLE 10-3. TEST SPECIFICATIONS FOR NATIONAL COUNCIL LICENSURE
EXAMINATION FOR REGISTERED NURSE LICENSURE**

Nursing Behavior	Locus of Decision Making
Assessing	Nurse-centered
Analyzing	Shared
Planning	Client-centered
Implementing	**Clinical Area**
Evaluating	Medical nursing
Cognitive Level	Surgical nursing
Knowledge	Obstetrical nursing
Comprehension	Psychiatric nursing
Application	Pediatric nursing
Analysis	

computer has received the response. At the conclusion of the test you may decide to share the score with the learner or design the test so that the score reports are given only to faculty.

Sequence. Sequence of elements or units in tests is limited to questions and learner response. If giving feedback, it should be done at the end of the test or the learner can be referred to remediation if necessary. The sequence of test items can be ordered, random, or adaptive. An *ordered* sequence is determined by the test designer and is based on the order in which the content was presented, the difficulty of the questions (easy to difficult), or any other logical reason for asking one question before another. Since questions in tests for health professionals are often based on application from a clinical example, there is usually a good rationale for an ordered sequence.

When content is learned for rote memory, such as anatomy or terminology, the sequence of test items is not crucial and you may wish to have questions generated by the computer randomly. *Random* test questions avert memorizing an order as opposed to meaning, and the use of these questions is one of the major values of using the computer for administering tests.

An *adaptive* sequence may be used if your test is measuring terminal objectives at a mastery level. Testing time is minimized as the learner can initially be tested at the highest level of mastery or returned to lower levels for review or remediation, as needed.

Learner Control. Learner control of pace and sequence is usually necessary in computer testing. As with paper and pencil tests, the testee should be able to review the entire test, access one screen at a time, and take as long as needed for each question.

Time. The time allocated for the test may be an important factor in test design. Time limits are typically placed on summative and standardized tests and should also be placed on similar examinations administered by the computer. Time limits are particularly necessary if you are comparing the results of paper and pencil tests with your computerized test.

- Determine time limits during test tryout.

SCREEN DESIGN

Attention must be given to screen design when developing a computer test. Input features must be included in the test design to overcome potential inabilities to scan the test and to change answers as can be done easily with paper and pencil tests.

To overcome the limits of single screen display, the learner should be able to page forward and backward. The learner should also understand how to enter the answer and be physically able to do so. This is particularly important when a light pen, mouse, or screen touch are used to enter answers.

To avoid test errors that reflect mechanical problems instead of lack of knowledge, the test must be designed so the learner has an opportunity to change the answers and verify responses before entering them (Fig. 10–2). A final entry key can also be used for this purpose.

Input errors can be minimized by keeping the keyboard entry for answers short. Using single digit numbers, or single letters (Y/N or T/F) is easier for the learner. If learners strike a key outside of the acceptable range (1 to 4, Y/N) the test program can be designed to provide a prompt that guides them to choose one of the acceptable options. An opportu-

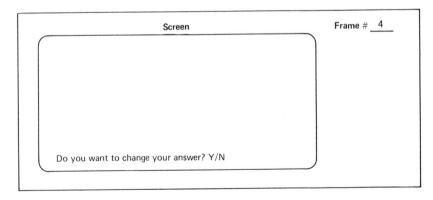

Figure 10–2. Screen design: Learner verification of response.

nity for response verification (Fig. 10-2) should also be designed for short answer questions.

Test items should be formatted for one test item per screen. Most authorities recommend using single-spacing for the stem of the question and using double-spacing for paragraphs and item options. The screen should be easy to read and should follow conventional test construction style.

Graphics are distracting during testing. They should only be used if they are the basis for a question.

TEST DESIGN

When constructing computer tests you should follow the same guidelines for developing paper and pencil tests (Table 10-4). The test should include directions, appropriate types of questions, test options, and scoring procedures. If statistical reports will be needed these should be determined at this time.

1. Directions. The directions for the test should appear in one of the first screens. They should be clearly written and explain exactly what is expected. Directions can include the purpose of the test, the type of test, the time limit, penalty for guessing, how to enter the response, and how to change a response (Fig. 10-3). Confine the directions to one screen if possible. If you cannot display the directions on one screen be certain the user can scroll forward and backward. Directions should also be accessible during the entire test.

2. Types of Tests. Although all types of tests can be administered on a computer, true/false and multiple choice tests are the easiest to construct. Matching items are slightly more difficult while fill-in-the-blank or free choice and essay tests require complex programming depending on the range of acceptable answers.

Clinical practicum tests can be administered with the computer, using adjuncts such as a mannequin or equipment used for a certain procedure. In this type of test the learner is directed to make observations about a client's condition or about the equipment and then return to the computer to respond to questions. Slides or videotapes can also be used as adjuncts to computer tests.

3. Test Questions. Test questions consist of a stem and, depending on the type of questions, various options from which the student is to select the correct answer. As stated earlier, test questions are derived from the lesson or course content and objectives.

TABLE 10-4. GUIDELINES FOR WRITING TEST ITEMS

Multiple Choice Tests

The *stem* should:
1. State the problem or question clearly
2. Contain only one thought or question
3. Be clearly written to minimize reading time

The *options* should:
1. Be sufficient to minimize effects of guessing; usually four
2. Contain only one correct answer
3. Be equal in length and form
4. Be based on information in the stem
5. Be free of qualifiers (generally, usually, often)
6. Be grammatically matched to the stem
7. Be plausible; clinically possible
8. Avoid use of "all of the above"; "none of the above"
9. Be written at a reading level of the least capable student
10. Vary in position of correct response
11. Be written in a logical order (range of high to low, alphabetically, first to last)

True/False Questions

The *stem* should:
1. Be limited to one fact, concept, procedure
2. Be written so the important part of the question is obvious

The *options* should:
1. Balance true and false answers
2. Avoid use of qualifiers (usually, generally)
3. Have clearly false answers (not false because "not" is added in front of a true statement)

Short Answer Questions

The *stem* should:
1. Clearly indicate the type of response to be given (number, formula, generic vs. trade name of a drug)
2. Be brief

The *response* should:
1. Be placed at the end of the stem
2. Be brief

Matching Questions

The *stem* should:
1. Be similar in context to the options
2. Be arranged in order (alphabetically, least to most)

The *options* should:
1. Be arranged in order
2. Be greater in number than the stems

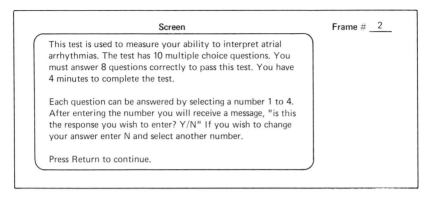

Figure 10-3. Screen design: Test directions.

Because the computer has capabilities for storing and sorting test questions it is possible to identify each question to assure balance when constructing the test. Each question could be identified by domain (cognitive, affective, psychomotor) cognitive level (comprehension, synthesis, etc.), content area, lesson or course objective, difficulty, step in a process, or page of text or reference source.

4. Item Options. The item options are the answers from which the student can choose (Table 10–4). Numbers are easier for students to use in responding to questions; use them for option selection.

5. Scoring. Before designing the test you should determine how the test will be scored. The use of a score to assign grades, for example, should be made known to the learner. Scoring results are usually given to the learner at the end of the test, but in some instances you may wish to display the ongoing score to the learner. If you plan to do this, be certain the test program is designed with this capability.

6. Statistical Reports. Item analysis and statistical reporting will give you information about your test and about the instruction that preceded it. This information will be useful to you when you assign grades and revise test items and instruction. If you are accustomed to receiving computer analysis of your tests from a test scoring center you will know how invaluable this information is. You may decide to include the number correct, percentage, mean, standard error of mean, standard deviation, Kuder Richardson reliability coefficient, standard error of measurement, item correlation, and difficulty level as statistical analyses of your test. If you share this information with the learner be certain he or she understands the interpretation of these statistics.

TRYOUT, REVISION, AND USE

If you have administered a paper and pencil test to groups of students, you already know the value of a tryout/revision cycle for tests. Who would ever guess the students could find so many test construction errors!

Revision and Use

To avoid these errors in *your* test, you can follow the tryout procedures suggested in Chapter 4. Before using the tests with the learners, have a colleague review the test for content and syntax errors. A colleague with test construction skills would also be a good person to review your test.

When the test has passed the first revision, try the test in paper and pencil form with a few of the students from the target audience and solicit their assessment of the clarity of the directions and the logic of the correct and incorrect answers. When the test is revised and coded for the computer you should once again try the test on the computer with several students.

As you use the test (particularly if it is a summative test used to assign grades or determine progression to another module) you must establish measures of reliability and validity (see Chap. 4). A final revision may still be needed, based on these determinations. The perfect test takes patience to develop, but it is worth the effort to be able to evaluate the outcomes of instruction.

Administering Computer Tests

Administering computer tests depends on the number of terminals, the number of students, and the nature of the test. You will need to consider each of these variables as you determine the best way for you and your students to use the computer for testing.

If you have enough computer terminals for each student to take the test at the same time, it will be possible for you to administer any test during an allocated test time. Because it is possible for the questions to be generated in a random order or to use alternative forms of the test, the opportunity for cheating can be controlled in this test setting.

When computer terminals are limited you may consider administering the test and alternative versions in a paper and pencil form and use the capabilities of the computer for generating the test, scoring, storing, reporting, and recording the results. Another possibility for administering the test on the computer is to stagger terminal use by assigning test appointments for each student. The likelihood that information will be shared by students is high in this setting, and, if test security is important it will be necessary to minimize sharing of information by close scheduling and by using alternative versions of the test.

Test Security

Tests that are used to monitor achievement and assign grades should be maintained as securely as possible. One way to safeguard tests is to incorporate user codes that allow access to the computer test and test bank to a limited number of individuals. The diskettes must also be stored in locked files in the same way that security is provided for paper and pencil tests.

SUMMARY

The computer is an ideal medium for administering tests. Summative, formative, adaptive, and computer managed tests can be developed for the computer. The main advantage of computer testing is the convenience for both the learner and teacher for self-administration and self-pacing. For some learners the computer can even improve test-taking skills and minimize test anxiety.

Computer tests are designed with the same care as paper and pencil tests. The design phases of product formulation, writing instructional specifications, and trying and revising the test before use should be followed. All traditional types of tests can be administered by the computer, but limited choice answers such as true/false, multiple choice, or short answer tests are easiest to construct. Adaptations are made in program design to assure that the test is measuring learner knowledge and not mechanical error. A checklist is provided at the end of the chapter to help you design CAI tests.

CHECKLIST: DESIGNING TESTS

Product formulation:

1. Development time allocated (25 to 50 hours)   _____
2. Test design consultant available   _____
3. Personnel available to develop CAI   _____
4. Test outline prepared   _____

Instructional specifications:

1. Needs analysis
   a. Type of test specified _____
   b. CAI best medium for test _____
2. Learner analysis
   a. Content mastered _____
   b. Experience with testing procedures _____
3. Task analysis
   a. Content identified _____
   b. Learning outcomes identified _____
   c. Test map (test specifications) developed _____
4. Purpose, goals, objectives
   a. Test meets purpose of instruction _____
   b. Objectives match test _____
5. Test designed using teaching–learning principles
   a. Feedback given at end of test _____
   b. Sequence of test questions is logical _____
   c. Adaptive testing procedures used for mastery learning _____
   d. Learner controls pace of questions _____
   e. Adequate time allowed to complete test _____

Screen design:

1. Screen pages forward and backward _____
2. Directions inform learner how to enter answer _____
3. Learner able to enter answer (use keyboard, other input devices) _____
4. Learner can correct/change answers _____
5. Error messages appear for input errors _____
6. One question per screen _____
7. Graphics support test _____

Test construction:

1. Directions
   a. Present _____
   b. Clear _____
   c. On one screen _____
   d. Can be referred to _____
2. Type of test appropriate to content _____
3. Test questions unambiguous _____
4. Test options
   a. Only one correct answer _____
   b. Unambiguous _____
5. Test scoring and reporting procedures present _____

G CAI COURSEWARE

any instructional medium, plans must be made to maximize use.
urseware must be incorporated into lesson plans and considera-
ust be given to arranging the elements of instruction, following
les of media use and making decisions about using CAI lessons
ndividuals or groups.

Lesson Plan

n plans are used by most teachers to identify the elements or events
struction, and the sequence of activities used to facilitate learning
p. 3). These may include gaining the learner's attention, establishing
etting for learning, facilitating learning, asking questions, giving
back and evaluating learning. CAI can be used to accomplish most
ese instructional elements, but is usually designed to accomplish
a few. The rest must be included by the instructor in the lesson plan.
When using CAI it is necessary to identify which elements of in-
ction can be met by the CAI lesson and which must be provided by
instructor. Drill and practice lessons, for example, only accomplish
elements, eliciting performance and providing feedback. The in-
ctor will, therefore, need to attend to gaining attention, establishing
learning environment, providing instruction and any other elements
ded by the learner. A lesson plan should be developed which indicates
v each element of instruction will be accomplished. Particular atten-
n should be given to accounting for elements of instruction *not* pro-
ed by the CAI courseware.

inciples of Media Use

ing CAI in the classroom should follow the same principles employed
en using any media. These include previewing the medium, preparing
e environment, preparing the learner, using the medium, and following
.

reviewing. The first step in using CAI is to preview the courseware
hap. 2). All course materials should be reviewed for content accuracy
nd operational effectiveness as well as for the relationship to the lesson
r course in which they will be used. The preview evaluation tool can be
sed to make notes for alerting the learners to points of interest.

Preparing the Environment. The next principle of media use is to pre-
are the enviromnent. If you will be using CAI in the classroom, be

Tryout, revision, and use:
1. Tryout includes:
   a. Learner   _____
   b. Subject matter expert   _____
   c. Test construction expert   _____
   d. Language expert   _____
2. Test revised before used   _____
3. Teacher's manual written   _____
4. Program documentation written   _____
5. Reliability and validity measures obtained
   a. Reliability   _____
   b. Validity   _____

REFERENCES

Brightman, H., Freeman, J., & Lewis, D. (1984). Constructing and using computer based formative tests. *Educational Technology, 24*(6), 36–38.
Kreitzberg, C., Stocking, M., & Swanson, L. (1984). Computerized adaptive
   testing: Principles and directions. In D. Walker & R. Hess (Eds.), *Instructional
   software: Principles and perspectives for design and use*. Belmont, Calif.:
   Wadsworth.
Reynolds, A. (1984). Using microcomputers in situational testing. *Nurse Educator, 9*(2), 39–42.
Wedman, J., & Stefanich, G. (1984). Guidelines for computer-based testing of
   student learning of concepts, principles and procedures. *Educational Technology, 24*(6), 23–28.
Weiss, D. (1979). Computerized adaptive achievement testing. In H. O'Neil (Ed.),
   Procedures for instructional systems development. New York: Academic Press.

Additional Readings

Bloom, B. (1956). *Taxonomy of educational objectives handbook I cognitive
   domain*. New York: D. McKay.
Landa, R. (1984). *Creating courseware*. New York: Harper & Row.
Mizokawa, D., & Hamlin, M. (1984). Guidelines for computer-managed testing.
   Educational Technology, 24(12), 12–17.

11

Using Computer A...
Instruction

*Computer assisted instruction is selected or designed fo...
ers, and once acquired, both teachers and students must...
using the courseware. After reading this chapter you wi...
corporate CAI courseware in your lesson plans and follo...
media use to prepare the learners and the environment. Y...
aware of the location, physical arrangements, and placer...
ment needed during courseware use.*

certain all learners will be able to see the screen or have an opportunity for individual time with the lesson. If courseware is used independently it is important that sufficient hardware is present and functional. If adjunct equipment is used with the lesson it should be ready.

Preparing the Learner. Prior to courseware use the learner should be informed about the purpose and objectives of the lesson. Learners should also know how they should use the courseware; for example, should they take notes? make a care plan? give a report to the instructor? take a test? If this is the only way the learner will have to obtain the content, the learner should also know if review opportunities will be available. Finally, the learner should be informed if he or she is being evaluated and if results are being reported to the instructor.

Preparation for CAI use can occur in a variety of ways. One approach is to write the information in a course syllabus. The information can also be shared verbally in class or as an information sheet distributed during class. In other instances the information may all be included in the CAI lesson itself.

The learner should also be prepared to use the computer (hardware), particularly when the courseware is assigned for independent use. Orienting the learner to the computer and computer use decreases anxiety and frustration (Kashka & Lease, 1984). A simple introductory program on using the computer can be designed or a demonstration given to the learner before use. Having instructions posted near the computer and user manuals available may be sufficient for some learners. Since adults learn from each other, orienting a few students who will then help others is another way to give support to students learning to use the computer.

Use. The next step is to use the CAI. Although most CAI courseware is designed to be used by learners independently of the instructor it can be advantageous to observe the first group of learners and evaluate their experience with the CAI lesson (Chap. 12).

Follow-up. Follow-up is the last, and often neglected, step of media use. Here the instructor provides the learner with an opportunity to validate learning and to debrief. In some teaching strategies, such as simulations, this step is particularly crucial. Follow-up can be done with a discussion, a written assignment, a questionnaire about the lesson's usefulness, or a posttest. It is important to be certain that the CAI courseware accomplished the learning objectives and that there is a sense of closure for the learners.

Individual or Group Use

When making plans about CAI use it is also important to determine whether the courseware will be used by individuals or groups. There are advantages and disadvantages that should be considered.

Use with Individuals. Since CAI is suited for independent study, self-paced learning, and can be used in an environment of privacy, most CAI can be used by individuals. When using the lesson with individuals it will be important for all learners to have equal-time access to the computer. This may involve using a system that can be transported to locations where the learners are (client's bedside, pharmacy, physician's office, nursing station) or to construct a centrally located learning resource center.

Use with Groups. Some CAI lessons are well suited to teams of students, small groups, or even a large group in a postclinical conference or classroom to give demonstrations, encourage group discussion, promote shared decision making, or peer tutoring. The computer can be used in a classroom with a large screen monitor or computer projector to increase visibility for large groups (Fig. 11-1). When CAI is used by groups of students in a learning resource center, the carrel should be flexible enough to accommodate several students and located so as not to disturb others.

THE COMPUTER LEARNING STATION

In order to use CAI it is necessary to locate the hardware where the learner can use it and arrange the learning station, or carrel, for comfort. Recent attention has been given to the human factors, or ergonomics,

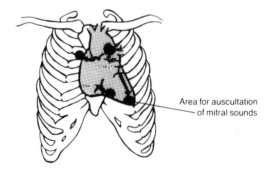

Area for auscultation of mitral sounds

Figure 11-1. Computer projector used to enlarge screen for classroom use of CAI.

in the design of the computer learning station. Factors such as location, physical arrangement, and equipment should be considered when designing the computer learning station.

Location

The computer learning station should be located conveniently. The location will depend on the number of users, the extent of CAI use, and the need for individual or group use.

When the number of users is small it is desirable to keep the learning station portable. A rolling cart can be used to transport the computer to a classroom or client's bedside.

More often, however, the number of users is large and it is advantageous to arrange a central location. This area should be in a location where students are likely to congregate such as near a library, classroom area, or a learning laboratory. Some libraries and learning resource centers have dedicated an area for computer use and have several carrels placed in one room.

The computer learning station should be arranged so that privacy can be obtained. Carrels with panels that can be opened to accommodate several students working together or closed to create privacy for individual learners are ideal.

Physical Arrangements

Attention is also given to the physical arrangements of the computer learning station. Provisions must be made for proper lighting, noise control, and electrical safety.

Lighting. The lighting for computer use is one third to one half less than needed for reading or viewing television (Yeaman, 1983). Lighting sources can be placed overhead and within the carrel (Fig. 11–2). Glare from direct light or bright indirect lighting causes eye fatigue and can be minimized by shading windows and painting walls in earth tones. Heat created by sunlight can also damage chips and warp disks and should be minimized. The brightness and contrast on the screen should be adjustable. If the learner is also reading at the carrel, additional spot lighting may be added.

Noise. Noise from printers, other students, adjunct audio, or keyboard use can be distracting to learners. Carrels should be separated and carpeted to absorb noise. Separate areas can be used for group study and talking.

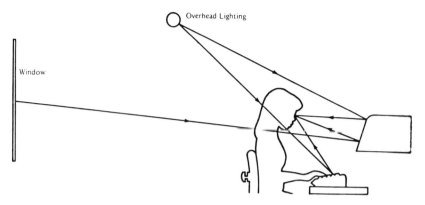

Figure 11-2. Lighting sources for CAI use. (From Yeaman, A. (1983). Microcomputer learning stations and student health and safety: Planning, evaluation and revision of physical arrangements. *Educational Technology, 12,* 16–21, with permission.)

Electrical Safety. When several computers are being used in one area the learning center should be wired to accommodate the energy load. Surge protectors should be used so that voltage spikes do not damage electrical components of the computer. Antistatic mats or carpeting should be used to decrease static electricity. Antistatic spray may be needed if ambient air is dry.

Equipment Placement

The keyboard, cathode ray tube (CRT, monitor), and chair must be arranged to avoid fatigue and muscle strain. Recommendations have been made by the National Institute of Occupational Safety and Health for workers who use computers. These same guidelines can be adapted for learners (Armstrong, 1984; Yeaman, 1983).

Chair. The chair used with the computer should have a five-prong base and an adjustable seat and backrest (Fig. 11-3). It should be selected for the size of the user (adult or child) and be able to be placed under the computer table with adequate leg clearance. A footrest can be used for short individuals (Fig. 11-3).

Monitor. The monitor should be placed above the keyboard in front of the learner. There should be one monitor for each keyboard so the learner does not strain to view the monitor when using a distant keyboard. The learner should be able to view the screen at about 18 to 20 inches at 10 to 20 degrees below eye level (Fig. 11-3). Adjustable shelves can be installed to provide this flexibility.

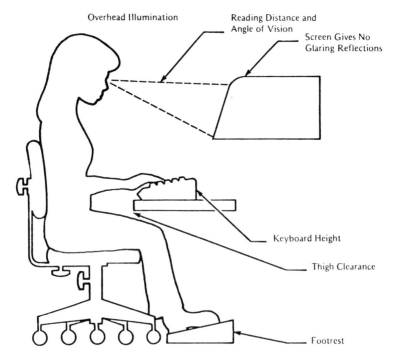

Figure 11-13. Learner position for using computer to avoid fatigue and muscle strain. Note position of chair and placement of monitor and keyboard. (From Yeaman, A. (1983). Microcomputer learning stations and student health and safety: Planning, evaluation and revision of physical arrangements. *Educational Technology, 12,* 16-21, with permission.)

Keyboard. The keyboard is placed at elbow height (Fig. 11-3). If the learner is using a workbook or other adjunct equipment, room should be provided in the carrel for these. The keyboard should be detachable so it can be positioned for the learner's comfort.

SUMMARY

CAI courseware is selected or designed to be used. Prior to use, however, plans must be made to incorporate the CAI lesson into a lesson plan, prepare for media use, and determine if the courseware will be used by individuals or groups. Arrangements must also be made to locate the computer where use is maximized. Physical arrangements include adequate lighting, noise control, and electrical safety. The chair, monitor, and keyboard should be placed with consideration for human factors of comfort and fatigue. Instructional effectiveness of CAI courseware is increased when the instructor makes these deliberate plans for use. These plans should be made while selecting or designing the courseware and implemented and evaluated on an ongoing basis.

REFERENCES

Armstrong, M. (1984). Ergonomic considerations in computer implementation: A primer. *Computers in Nursing, 2*(4), 121–124.

Kashka, M., & Lease, B. (1984). A design for the development of a computer assisted instruction tutorial module. *Computers in Nursing, 2*(4), 136–142.

Yeaman, A. (1983). Microcomputer learning stations and student health and safety: Planning, evaluation and revision of physical arrangements. *Educational Technology, 12*, 16–21.

Additional Readings

Coburn, P., Kelman, P., Robert, A., et al. (1982). *Practical guide to computers in education.* Reading, Mass.: Addison-Wesley.

Feeg, V. (1984). The computer education challenge to nursing education. What? When? How? and Why? *Computers in Nursing, 2*(3), 88–91.

Kadner, K. (1984). Change: Introducing computer-assisted instruction (CAI) to a college of nursing faculty. *Journal of Nursing Education, 23*(8), 349–350.

Kearsley, G., & Hillelshor, M. (1982). Human factors considerations for computer-based training. *Journal of Computer-Based Instruction, 8*(4), 74–84.

Roblyer, M. D. (1983). Toward more effective microcomputer courseware through application of systematic instructional design methods. *AEDS Journal, 17*(102), 23–32.

Townsend, B., & Hale, D. (1981). Coping strategies for resistance to microcomputers. *Technological Horizons in Education Journal, 8*(6), 49–52.

12

Evaluating Computer Assisted Instruction

I. CAI Evaluation
   A. Levels of Evaluation
   B. CAI Evaluators
   C. Methods and Tools
II. Evaluating Courseware
III. Evaluating Use
IV. Evaluating Learning Outcomes

Evaluation is an ongoing component of lesson, course, and curriculum development and evaluation of CAI should be an integral component of these evaluation plans. After reading this chapter you will be able to recognize three levels of CAI evaluation, identify appropriate evaluators, and use evaluation methodology and tools for CAI evaluation. You will also be able to evaluate courseware, CAI use, and learning outcomes.

CAI EVALUATION

CAI evaluation is conducted to make decisions about use. Evaluators are concerned with CAI effectiveness and can decide to continue to use CAI, develop or purchase more CAI, expand CAI facilities, and, if necessary, abandon CAI as a medium of instruction. When evaluating CAI it is helpful to specify what is being evaluated, who is conducting the evaluation, and what are the methodology and tools used to gather evaluative data.

Levels of Evaluation

CAI evaluation can be described as taking place at three levels (Reeves & Lent, 1984). The first level is evaluating the courseware itself. The focus is on the courseware content and design. At the second level evaluators examine courseware use. The emphasis here is on the interactions of the user, the courseware, and the hardware. Evaluation efforts must also be directed to examine learning outcomes when CAI is used as a medium of instruction. This evaluation examines the long-term impact on CAI and learning.

CAI Evaluators

CAI evaluation can and should be conducted by all persons involved in CAI development and use. Evaluators therefore may be CAI authors, instructional designers, programmers, faculty, students, administrators, health care service personnel, and media services (learning resource center) personnel. Each has a vested interest in the success of CAI and should be included in evaluation efforts and apprised of the results.

Methods and Tools

A variety of evaluation methods and tools is used to evaluate the CAI courseware, its use, and the learning outcomes. Naturalistic evaluation methods may be used to identify values for CAI as a medium of instruction, user needs, and use (Billings, 1984). Goals-based methods of evaluation may be used to determine effectiveness of CAI development projects (Worthen & Sanders, 1973).

A variety of tools can be used to collect evaluation data. These may include checklists, rating scales, behavioral observation, anecdotal notes, and learner self-reports.

EVALUATING COURSEWARE

Courseware evaluation involves making judgments about the CAI lesson. The evaluator verifies content accuracy, instructional specifications, use of teaching–learning principles, instructional strategy, lesson design, screen design, and lesson operation, as well as documentation and adjunct learning aids. An anecdotal record, checklist, or rating scale can be used to record courseware evaluation (Chap. 2).

Information obtained from courseware evaluation is shared with lesson developers, potential courseware users, and administrators who make decisions about purchasing courseware. Courseware reviews should remain on file in a central location where others may use them.

EVALUATING USE

In addition to evaluating courseware it is also important to evaluate CAI use. Use evaluation, or operational testing, involves collecting data about the extent of use, time of use, as well as ease of use. Information from use evaluation is shared with faculty, learning resource center personnel, and administrators to support requests (or no requests) for additional software, hardware, and learning laboratories. Use evaluation is also reported to lesson developers to indicate need (or no need) for further lesson revision.

Records should be maintained to document media use. Information should be collected about the course or program in which the CAI was used, the type of user (basic student, continuing education student, client, faculty), how the CAI was used (individual, group, classroom, home), the number of users, the learner's subjective responses to the lesson as well as objective data from lesson scores and other test scores such as unit or final examinations, and clinical practice evaluations or certification or licensure examinations (Fig. 12-1).

Learning resource centers may be interested in determining the time of day the courseware is used and how long each learner spends with the lesson. A use log can be developed to gather these data (Fig. 12-2). Use records can also be incorporated in the CAI lesson.

Observation of learners using the courseware reveals important information about courseware operations. Data can be collected about the learner's response to the program, the ease of operations, the clarity of directions, and the ability of a student to use the lesson independently. Use observations can be recorded as anecdotal notes (Fig. 12-3). These

---

MEDIA USE EVALUATION

Date:

Time:

Courseware Title:

Course or Program Used in:

Type of Learner:

How Used (group, individual):

Learner's Response:

Lesson Data:
    (scores)

Correlation With Other Test Scores:

Figure 12-1. Media use evaluation tool.

DATE	TIME OUT	IN	USER NAME	STATUS FACULTY/STUDENT	COMMENTS

Figure 12-2. CAI use log.

records can be made by learners, faculty, or learning resource center assistants and should include information about the problem and the corrective action required.

Use data can also be obtained by noting the learner's attitudes and opinions about CAI, the computer, and the lesson. Self-reports or questionnaires can be designed to obtain this information (Table 12-1).

EVALUATING LEARNING OUTCOMES

When CAI is used as a medium of instruction it is important to determine how CAI contributed to the instructional needs and the learner's achieve-

Date: Time:

Description of Incident:

Action Taken:

Name of Observer:

Figure 12-3. Anecdotal record—CAI courseware use.

TABLE 12-1. COURSEWARE USER'S EVALUATION

Directions: Please assist us to evaluate this CAI program by completing the following questionnaire. Deposit the questionnaire in the box provided in learning lab.

	Strongly Agree	Agree	Undecided	Disagree	Strongly Disagree

ABOUT THE COMPUTER:

1. I enjoy using the computer.
2. The computer is difficult for me to use.
3. I was adequately instructed about using the computer before I used this CAI program.
4. Using the computer helps me learn.
5. I prefer using the computer to attending a lecture class.
6. The computer was available for use when I needed it.
7. The computer "breaks down" frequently.
8. I needed to ask for help to use the computer.
9. I prefer using the computer to study at my own pace.
10. Someone was available to help me use the computer.
11. I wish the computer center was open at different hours.

ABOUT THE CAI LESSON:

1. The directions for using this lesson were clear.
2. I never could follow the lesson.
3. This lesson was too difficult for me.
4. I would rather learn this content in a lecture class.
5. I was able to understand the content of this lesson.
6. This lesson was challenging for me.
7. I really understand the content of the lesson now.
8. This lesson took too much time to learn the content.
9. The content of this lesson is practical.
10. The content of this lesson will help me be a better nurse.
11. This lesson bored me.

ment of learning outcomes. These outcomes are reflected in course evaluations and learner examination scores.

Since the CAI lesson was developed to meet an instructional need, it is useful to verify that the need has been met. Did learners learn the content more effectively or efficiently? Was faculty time used more productively as a result of students learning from the CAI? Answers to these questions appear as faculty perform course evaluations.

CAI is also used to assist learners meet course objectives as documented by pre- and posttests and unit examinations. These examinations may be included in the CAI lesson. Administering a test 2 to 6 weeks after CAI use is useful to determine knowledge retention. Simulations are recommended as another evaluation strategy to validate retention at the application level (Reeves & Lent, 1984).

Impact evaluation is used to determine the long-term effects of CAI as a medium of instruction. Here data are collected about changes in learner's clinical practice, efficiency in the work setting after a training program, or (when used for client instruction) compliance with self-care, or postprocedure/postsurgery recovery. Other long-term measurements are obtained from results on standardized tests such as state board licensure examinations or certification examinations.

SUMMARY

Evaluation is the final step of CAI product development and use, and is conducted to make decisions about effectiveness. Evaluation activities focus on the courseware itself, courseware use, and the long-term impact on learning outcomes. A variety of evaluation methods and tools can be used to gather evaluative data which are ultimately shared with CAI authors, instructional designers, programmers, faculty, administrators, health care service personnel, and learning resource center administrators.

REFERENCES

Billings, D. (1984). A model for evaluating computer assisted instruction. *Nursing Outlook, 32,* 50–53.

Reeves, T., & Lent, R. (1984). Levels of evaluation for computer-based instruction. In D. Walker, & R. Hess (Eds.), *Instructional software: Principles and perspectives for design and use.* Belmont, Calif.: Wadsworth.

Worthen, B., & Sanders, J. (1973). *Education evaluation: Theory and practice.* Belmont, Calif.: Wadsworth.

Additional Readings

Broich, G., & Jemelka, R. (1981). Evaluation. In H. O'Neil (Ed.), *Computer-based instruction: A state of the art assessment*. New York: Academic Press.

Hakansson, J. (1982). How to evaluate educational courseware. *Journal of Courseware Review*, *1*(1), 3–5.

Walker, D., & Hess, R. (Eds.). (1984). Evaluation in courseware development. In *Instructional software: Principles and perspectives for design and use*. Belmont, Calif.: Wadsworth.

Wallace, J., & Rose, R. (1984). A hard look at software: What to examine and evaluate (with an evaluation form). *Educational Technology*, *24*(10), 35–39.

Glossary

Advance control. Movement of screen forward or backward; use controlled by user.

Artificial intelligence. Capability of computer to be programmed to perform functions associated with human intelligence, such as logical thinking or reasoning.

Authoring language. Type of programming language used to simplify and reduce time needed to develop CAI lessons.

Authoring system. (Author-prompting system) Program designed to create other programs, namely CAI lessons.

Authoring tools. Languages and programs used to facilitate development of CAI; includes programming language, authoring language, authoring systems, text editors, graphics editors, and instructional design systems.

Blueprint. Overview of the lesson; usually includes a graphic representation as well as a narrative.

Branching programs. Decison points for alternative selections of action. In a simulation, branching represents alternative courses for action; in a tutorial, branching represents alternatives for study.

Cathode ray tube (CRT). Video display monitor; screen used to display text and graphics.

Central processing unit (CPU). Circuits that control and execute instructions; contains the internal memory, control unit, and arithmetic logic unit; directs the computer and peripheral devices.

Code. Meaning assigned to characters or symbols.

Coding. Process of translating flowchart or storyboard into code.

Computer assisted instruction. General term indicating use of computer for instruction.

Computer assisted learning. General term used to emphasize use of computer for learning.

Computer based training. Use of computer to manage instruction; emphasis is on training settings and training tasks.

Computer managed instruction. Use of computer to manage instruction; emphasis is on directing student's progress, maintaining records, and producing progress reports for students and instructors.

Concept analysis. Process of identifying the components of a concept; breaking concept into criterial attributes and irrelevant attributes and placing the components in a logical order for instruction.

Courseware. Computer programs to teach or train; focus is on instructional objectives and learning outcomes.

Debug. Locate and remove errors in lesson design, flowcharts, or coded lessons.

Default value. Value automatically used by system when there are no specific instructions given.

Developmental testing. First tryout of the lesson draft by content expert, language expert, and learner.

Disk. External storage medium; magnetic surface used to store data.

Disk drive. Device to which data can be written or from which data can be read; device used to store data on disk.

Documentation. Written manuals used to communicate specific information about the courseware to the instructor and learner; also refers to user information about hardware and software needed to use the lesson.

Drill and practice. Instructional strategy in which learner practices learning for mastery.

Error message. Information given on the screen to the learner that input or response is not acceptable.

Feedback. Information given to the learner about his or her response.

Field testing. Final courseware evaluation; conducted by different learners or the same learners in different settings.

Flowchart. Graphic representation of problem and problem solution; used to diagram the lesson overview and guide computer programming.

Gaming. Instructional strategy that features competition and a win element.

Graphics. Animation, drawings, graphs, pictures used to enhance instruction.

Hardware. Physical equipment of the computer system; includes CRT, disk drive, keyboard, CPU, input/output devices.

Input device. Hardware used to enter data in computer; includes keyboard, mouse, joystick, light pen, touch screen.

Instructional specifications. Statements of instructional intentions; includes needs analysis, learner analysis, knowledge analysis, purpose, goals, and objectives.

Instructional strategy. Form of instruction used to obtain learning outcomes; common strategies for CAI are drill and practice, tutorial, simulation, and testing.

Intelligent computer assisted instruction. Courseware with capabilities of diagnosing learner problems and presenting varied instruction based on learner's responses.

Interactive video. Combination of the computer and videodisk or videotape for instructional purposes; features the interactivity of the computer and the motion and realism of the video.

Internal memory. Internal storage of computer.

Inverse video. Background and foreground colors reversed to highlight words on the screen (also called reverse video).

Knowledge analysis. Process used to identify the domain of knowledge to be used in instruction and the structure of the knowledge.

Learner analysis. Process used to identify the attributes of the learner relevant to the design of the instruction.

Learner control. Design feature in instruction that permits the learner to choose level and amount of instruction.

Learning outcomes. Expected performance of the learner after instruction.

Light pen. Input device to touch the screen (CRT) to add, change, or delete information on the screen.

Linear programs. Lessons with unidirectional paths; all learners follow the same course of instruction; in simulations all learners are directed to the same course of action.

Memory. Location where data is stored; internal memory is stored in CPU.

Menu. List of choices from which the user can make a selection; includes course menus, lesson menus, and authoring menus.

Modem. Device used to connect data processing devices for transmission, usually over telephone lines.

Monitor. Video display device; the screen (CRT).

Needs analysis. Process of identifying the need for instruction that can be met by a learning experience.

Network. Interconnection of computer systems by data communications facilities.

Output. Data transferred from internal memory of the computer to an output device.

Output device. Devices used to transport information from the computer to the user; includes CRT, tape, disk, disk drives, printers.

Paging. Movement of one screen to the next.

Peripheral device. Equipment controlled by CPU; includes printers, videodisks, videotapes, audiotapes, CRT, screen displays, modems.

Pilot testing. Second testing of lesson; lesson tested with the target audience.

Pixel. Dots of light; *pic*ture *el*ement, determines resolution.

Program. Instructions telling the computer operations to perform.

Programming language. Tool used by author or programmer to communicate with the computer.

Prompt. Message on screen informing learner of action to pursue, such as enter a response or correct a response.

Reliability. Extent to which the courseware is dependable and predictable for different groups of learners.

Resolution. Density and quality of video display; the numbers of points or pixels on CRT.

Scroll. Move video display up or down in continuous motion; can be automatic or controlled by user.

Simulation. Instructional strategy that creates an imitation of a real-life process or situation.

Software. Programs that carry out the computer operations.

Storyboard. Mechanism for representing each screen display; screen design drafted on a small card that can be edited and rearranged before coding the lesson.

Systems software. Computer programs supplied by the computer manufacturer to operate the computer and peripheral devices, such as a disk operating system or input/output programs.

Task analysis. Process of identifying the steps of a skill or learning task; involves identifying the main task, breaking it into subtasks, and identifying associated learning sequences.

Text. Words on the screen.

Tutorial. Instructional strategy featuring questions and responses with individualized tutoring.

Validity. Extent to which courseware represents reality.

Index

Figures are indicated by *f*; tables are indicated by *t*.